D1602376

DEMOCRACY
AND
ETHNIC DIVERSITY
IN NIGERIA

Joseph A. Umoren

University Press of America, Inc.
Lanham • New York • London

Copyright © 1996 by
Joseph A. Umoren
University Press of America,® Inc.
4720 Boston Way
Lanham, Maryland 20706

3 Henrietta Street
London, WC2E 8LU England

Library of Congress Cataloging-in-Publication Data

Umoren, Joseph A.
Democracy and ethnic diversity in Nigeria / Joseph A. Umoren.
p.   cm.
Includes bibliographical references and index.
1. Nigeria--Ethnic relations. 2. Ethnicity--Nigeria. 3. Democracy--
Nigeria. 4. Nigeria--Politics and government--1960- I. Title.
DT515.42.U46   1996   305.8'009669--dc20   96-10673 CIP

ISBN 0-7618-0298-3 (cloth: alk. ppr.)

❦

DEDICATION

To all Nigerians and democracy worldwide

and

To my late parents,
Chief Aaron and Madam Cecilia Umoren
in memory of the civic and evangelical duties
they rendered to their community.

❦

Contents

List of Tables, Illustrations and Maps

Preface

The overall objective of this book is to help our readers have a glimpse of Nigeria and its past and present socio–political problems. It is also about a nation in transition. Heavy emphasis is placed on the economic crossroad of democracy and ethnicity to include the effect of poor social and political management on a pluralistic society. The entire text is research–oriented, prepared for Nigerians and their well wishers by a Nigerian, who by virtue of his nationality, strongly advocates a stable democratic government in Nigeria. In essence, the book is about what we are, and what we could have been.

Through the review of different aspects of Nigeria's historical past, much of the information therein is aimed at making a sociological discovery having some political and economic implications to Nigeria. Additionally, there are similarities in social, cultural characteristics and political realities between Nigeria and other countries in Africa. Their similarities have not only broadened the horizon of this presentation, but have also created the basis for intra–continental generalization. Our commitment to call a spade a spade in this investigation is guided by an impeccable scholarly principle, and serves only as a means of maintaining our clarity of purpose. As grim as some parts of this episode may be, they are specifically guarded by the events that created them and of the "truth that shall set us all free."

Accordingly, it is only when human beings seek "honesty as the best policy," and "honest" solutions to their life situations, that honest solutions can be found. This lesson was aptly taught by the 36th

President of the United States named Lyndon Baines Johnson (LBJ) who in the 1960's showed great moral courage when America was confronted with grave domestic problems. Following the tragic death of President Kennedy and a depressed economy, LBJ announced to his people that the "state of the union was not good" and proceeded to the job of nation building. President Johnson's presidency is remembered by such high achievements as "signing $11.5 billion tax reduction and the Civil Rights bills, proclaimed war on poverty and being elected to a full presidential term." (The New Lexicon Webster Dictionary of the English Language 1989, PR-23).

Likewise, Nigerian Leaders as well as all African leaders can be required to show moral leadership in recognizing and providing remedies to tribalism, political and social instability, and economic decay in their societies. Recognizing, as well as solving national problems forthrightly is the only step to dynamize a society and maintain its national sovereignty. Even though the viewpoints and statements as contained in the pages of this book may elicit controversies and rightly so, the motivation to write what we feel remains the same. It is realized that a loss of national sovereignty begins not only in the capitulation to foreign interests or submission to selfish ambitions, but also in the resignation of citizens in matters of nationalism.

The future of Nigeria's political and socio-economic stability depends on what happens here onward. Such stability relates to lifestyle changes and learning new habits which are faraway from the dependence on internal gimmicks and external praetorianism. Like the prodigal son in the Bible, Nigeria can restore itself to peace and prosperity only when it falls in step with the wishes and tradition of its ancestors, starting with the homecoming decision and reconciliation.

"I will rise and go to my father and I will say unto him, Father I have sinned against heaven and before thee..." (Lk 15:18-24). All Nigerians from North to South, East to West must conciliate with their fatherland, one kindred and another.

Joseph A. Umoren Ph.D., December 1, 1995

Scope of the Text

The entire text is composed of seven easy–to–read chapters. Chapter One sets the stage by giving the reader a broad perspective of issues relating to Nigeria's social, political and economic environment. It presents to the reader pertinent appetizing information which otherwise would have been swept under the rug or treated as insignificant as Nigeria contemplates its political reform.

The importance of Chapter Two is to provide a linkage between the current work and related theories as a basis for understanding human behavior within the framework of a pluralistic society. Chapter Three globalizes the issue of ethnicity, human rights and prejudices, democracy and national unity to develop a comparison between Nigeria and other countries in matters of ethnic relations. Chapter Four describes the early European and Arab invasion and occupation of Africa into Nigeria's region. It delineates the socio–economic, political and religious implications of the respective spheres of influence in the Nigeria's southern and northern territories, and the subsequent amalagmation of these territories into one Nigeria.

In Chapter Five, the historical origin of Nigerians is developed from the biblical, sociological and ethnological perspectives raising the questions of social heterogeneity and political instability therefrom. Chapters Six and Seven are devoted to the detailed discussion of specific issues such as political instability, corruption, religion, language, tribalism, and foreign influence as they affect Nigeria's national integration and development. Additionally, in Chapter Seven the issue of democracy is discussed not only delineating Nigeria's continual difficulty in this area but also offering concrete proposals for the future of Nigeria's democracy as well as the role of its military.

Acknowledgments

I wish to thank my wife, Mrs. Deborah Umoren and my children, Ima–Obong Umoren and Uduak–Abasi Umoren for their patience and moral support. I also want to thank Ms. Kathy Mizzer, my typist, who was very accommodating of me during the typing process. Finally, to Mr. Melaku Tefera who helped me to artistically express some of the contents of the book.

Chapter One

Introduction

From time immemorial, there have been persistent myths, mis-
steps as well as expectations about postcolonial Nigeria and its
economic, social and political existence. These perceptions tend to relate
to the abundance of natural resources on one hand and the appearance
of dismal national consciousness, leadership and economic under
achievement on the other. When referring to the overall look of things,
"appearance" is in fact a weak word to describe Nigeria today. Even
though it may be difficult to accept it, most people are even beginning
to believe that things were better before Nigerians started governing
themselves. They would contend that prior to 1960, they had: year
round schools to attend, enough food to eat; a government, though
managed by foreigners, that was predictable; families that had self
worth; and a "country" that was respected abroad. Specifically, the
crucial problems facing Nigeria are those relating but not limited to the
following:

1. Nigeria's social, political and economic well being;
2. Individual freedom, human rights and freedom of the press as
   measured by democratic principles and the rule of law, and;
3. Nigeria's continual existence as one nation under the prevalent
   political chaos.

Answers to the above problems demand that Nigerians of all walks of life engage in some soul-searching activities taking into consideration Nigeria's dismal performance in domestic and world politics as well as in social and economic development. It is expected that Nigeria, at some point, would be able to decide the best political and economic systems for itself. But the effectiveness of such a decision would depend on the ability of Nigerian policymakers to acknowledge or discern the discrepancy existing between the actual and the ideal political, social and economic shape of the nation. Generally, policymakers are change agents who must have the correct dose of conviction and vision to perform their task successfully. Like Nelson Mandela, it was that deep conviction against apartheid and political oppression in South Africa that emboldened him to struggle for democracy and racial equality. When that struggle against apartheid ended on May 10, 1994, it was replaced by a democratic elected government. As the new president, Mr. Mandela, stated, "Never, never and never again shall this beautiful land experience the oppression of one by another and suffer the indignity of being the skunk of the world" (Taylor, 1994, A1.). During his revisit to the United States and the United Nations on October 3, 1994, Mandela reiterated his vision for South Africa from the standpoint of its leadership. He said, "For a leader to live a life unrelated to that of the people he serves is unacceptable." With these proverbial statements, Mandela could have been having Nigeria in mind as well.

We do not intend to beat Mr. Mandela's drum too loudly but it is fair to say that in the minds of many people, he is an example of the type of a moral leader that Africa in general and Nigeria in particular needs. He was energized throughout his life believing that South Africa could do better. But as Mandela is addressing the issues of racial oppression in South Africa, no one should lose sight of the greater danger posed by tribalism and tribal oppression now viewed by most people as the most subtle destroyer of prospects of democracy in almost all parts of Africa. The issue of tribes and democracy in Africa, so far neglected, deserves a serious look. It is our intention to tackle this issue in some detail in the succeeding pages.

In recent years, most people have attributed Nigeria's social, economic and political failure to various etiological factors. Dr. Okoh's suggestion to "Rotate the Presidency Every Two Years," was therefore an attempt to quell tribal dominance in Nigerian politics. He also blamed Nigeria's political instability on lack of a workable national

NIGERIA: SOCIAL, ECONOMIC AND DEMOGRAPHIC DATA

YEAR	PER CAPITA INCOME IN U.S. $	POPULA-TION ESTIMATE IN MILLIONS	BIRTH RATE PER 1,000 POP.	DEATH RATE PER 1,000 POP.	% OF URBAN POPUL-ATION	% OF POPU-LATION UNDER 15	% OF POPU-LATION OVER 65
1984	860	88.1	49	17	28	48	2
1985	760	91.2	48	17	28	48	2
1986	770	105.4	48	18	28	48	2
1987	760	108.6	46	18	28	45	2
1988	640	111.0	46	17	28	45	2
1989	370	115.3	46	17	28	45	2
1990	290	118.8	46	17	31	45	2

Source: World Population Data Sheet, Population Reference Bureau, Inc. Washington, D.C.

constitution. This view can be interpreted to mean that, even though Nigeria has a constitution, it has not been put to use or respected. He was perhaps referring to the 1989 Constitution. He advocated powersharing at the federal level of government as a means of unifying the different segments of society. His opinion about the 1994 proposed constitutional conference as contained in his summary statement that: "Nigeria by its size and natural resources can put its own house in order. We already have a constitution but apparently it is not working" (Okoh, 1994, 14).

While this political scientist is somewhat correct in most of his assessment relative to both the existing constitution and the proposed constitutional conference under Gen. Sani Abacha, there is need to investigate why constitutions, no matter how inclusive they may be, do not work in Nigeria. We need to also investigate why Nigerians seem to condone the unusual fashion by which constitutions are declared null and void whenever "a new cock visits the village." Unless this unpatriotic behavior is curbed, it can be easily predicted that Nigeria may never have a working constitution or survive as a nation–state. A constitution is often regarded as the lifeline of every civilized society. Usually, it is treated with the highest respect and irreproachableness once it has been accepted. As U.S. President Gerald Ford advised in his January 12, 1977 State of the Union Address, "the constitution is the bedrock of our freedom, guard and cherish it; keep honor and order in your own house; and the republic will endure." Yet, another U.S. President, James Buchanan on May 23, 1956 wrote, "there is nothing stable but Heaven and the Constitution."

In order to solve the sociopolitical problem in Nigeria, it is important to differentiate its symptoms from its illnesses. Treating the symptoms of Nigeria's illnesses; sometimes by only bandaging them, has always been a costly national mistake for many years. We predict that once the most notorious illness of Nigeria's political life is treated, many Nigerians are likely to discover that most of today's constitutional conferences have not only been gimmicks but wasted efforts. Most were delaying tactics by the powerholders to hang onto power at the expense of overall national well–being. There is enough evidence, therefore, that the problem of Nigeria's disunity may not lie in the constitution per se but in Nigerians themselves. Men determine the laws that govern them. After the laws are determined, citizens are required

Education for social change and civil liberty. . .

A need for moral leadership. . .

to stick with the laws by making them work and by civilly and democratically amending the laws to meet the needs of society.

In history, it is not uncommon that disputes over national constitutions have existed at the initial stages of national development. For example, the Constitution of the United States "was drafted by the Constitutional Convention of May 25–Sept. 17, 1787, and following its ratification by a convention in two–thirds of the states as provided in the constitution, became effective in 1789" (Morse 1970, 2368). But the Civil War in the United States that challenged the constitution did not occur until 1860–1865. This Civil War was fought primarily to stop the southern states from seceding from the Union and to preserve the integrity of the U.S. Constitution.

The most affected part of the Constitution at that time was the 14th Amendment which affirmed that "all men are created equal." The Southern states which had benefitted from slavery wanted it to continue. The Northern states wanted to abolish it in reference to the December 6, 1865 ratified 13th Amendment of the Constitution, stating that "neither slavery nor involuntary servitude, except as a punishment for crime whereof the party shall have been duly convicted, shall exist within the United States or any place subject to their jurisdiction." The disagreement between the South and North resulted in the Confederate forces attack on Fort Sumter in Charleston, South Carolina, setting off the Civil War in the United States. President Abraham Lincoln moved quickly to mobilize the Union forces which defeated the Confederate forces to preserve both the Union and the Constitution. So in 1863, Lincoln formally issued the Emancipation Proclamation and freed the slaves. Since then the United States has been observed as enjoying, though not without racial struggle along the way, a consistent social and economic development that places it as a great nation today.

The morals of this piece of historical documentary are twofold: firstly, it suggests that in almost every phase of national development, there are ups and downs, mistakes to be made, lessons to be learned and yet repeats of future mistakes to be avoided. Secondly, that Nigeria's political problems are rooted in something deeper than mere misunderstanding or disagreement between peoples on strong national issues. If Nigeria's problem had a simple solution, the Civil War of 1967 would have corrected it. There tends to be no similarity between Nigeria and the United States in this regard, or the constitutional question. Insofar as Nigeria has had numerous constitutional conferences since 1922 without any favorable outcome vis–a–vis the unity of

Nigeria, there is room for the public to be cynical about their patriotic intentions in the future. In 1994, when Gen. Sani Abacha called for another constitutional conference, it became unpopular and made the possibility of a democratic government in Nigeria somewhat tentative for obvious reasons. For millions of Nigerians who before November 18, 1993, had heralded the arrival of an elected government in Nigeria, the replacement of Shonekan – the interim civilian administrator – by Sani Abacha, represented a move "to erase any trace of democracy" in Nigeria (Fritz 1993, A9).

With that episode, beginning with the annulment of June 1993 presidential election by Gen. Babangida, the world was also eager to know what necessitated the delay to install the duly elected government of Mr. Abiola. From many quarters, there was a demand to know what Gen. Abacha had to offer Nigeria that would be different from what Gen. Babangida had already offered it. With all the political maneuvers, it seemed not too many people, although keeping their fingers crossed, were convinced that Gen. Abacha would offer anything new to Nigeria except the promise that "they [the military] believe that Nigeria deserves better" (Aigbogun, 1993, A13). It should also be noted that Gen. Abacha did not replace Shonekan as most historians may attempt to report. This would be a bad history lesson. Shonekan was only an innocent fill–in bystander who was manipulated by a higher power base. After all, "Mr. Shonekan was widely believed to be a puppet of general Abacha" (Aigbogun 1993, A13). Some political analysts have already maintained that handing over power to the civilian in a democratic process was never intended and that future democracy in Nigeria was utopian–thinking. What was meant to happen however, was the replacement of Gen. Babangida, who seemed to have run out of new gimmicks to maintain the nation's continued militocracy.

Militocratic institutions and ideologies were believed to have been formulated beginning in 1985 by Gen. Abacha's military predecessor, Gen. Babangida. Other tangential policies by the military had therefore come to be regarded often as "a facade to create the illusion of returning Africa's most populous nation to democracy" (Fritz 1993, A9). In order to retain power, Gen. Babangida's particular stock in trade was to keep the nation in suspense by constant shifting of his cabinet members under his self–styled "general 'demilitarization process' of Nigeria's political life" (Babarinsa, Mohammed, Akinrinade, Oludepo, Mba, Ben 1990, 15). Babarinsa (1990) gave a somewhat detailed summary of Gen. Babangida's term in office when he stated that

"General Ibrahim Babangida is the first Nigerian leader to employ instability as a conscious instrument of state policy" (p.18). It is however noteworthy that when Gen. Babangida first took power from Gen. Buhari in August of 1985, he was well received by the people as the lesser of two evils. His regime came when most Nigerians were already discontented with what came to be regarded as "meaningless coup d'etat" in Nigeria. Gen. Babangida's apparent show of patriotism came in 1986 when he initially rebuffed the International Monetary Fund (IMF) and the World Bank for what seemed unfair financial policies towards Nigeria – the structural Adjustment Program (SAP). Gen. Babangida's action might have been justified at that time. Most African countries depended on IMF and World Bank loans. But their conditions were detrimental to African health care, educational and infrastructure developments. The UN Secretary–General's report on the Implementation of the Africa Recovery Programme, A Summary: confirmed that "the significant policy reforms and structural adjustment measures by African countries have often entailed severe social costs and formidable political risks" (United Nations, 1987,3). Countries benefiting from these loans were mandated to concentrate only on economic activities which would enhance repayment of foreign loans. African critics argued that while belt tightening under the current SAP was a sound economic idea, it had the potential to stifle African growth and development.

As could have been expected, Babangida's action to redeem Nigeria economically was short lived. His "home grown Adjustment Programme" (Smith 1990, 7) had become the worst nightmare to Nigeria's economy. Unfortunately, at this time it was difficult for Nigerians to adjust to a lifestyle of self denial as suggested by SAP after being used to the extravagance and wasteful spending of the oil boom years. Most people maintained that SAP encouraged smuggling of goods into Nigeria which only benefitted the wealthy elites. The poor had to struggle under the so–called austerity measures which seemed to promote corruption at all levels of society. In spite of the ensuring economic and social bleakness in the country, Gen. Babangida had supporters who felt he was taking the country in the right direction.

Ugochukwu (1986, 1567) stated that "several years of economic recession appeared to have been halted by the end of 1985 when President Ibrahim Babangida announced Nigeria's budget which aimed to restructure and diversify the productive base of the economy...." His plan was to "run in parallel to the crowded political programme of return to civilian role in 1992" (Smith 1990, 6). But neither Nigeria's economy nor the general living standard of Nigerians had improved during Babangida's term. Above all, in 1994, Nigeria was still under the dictatorship of the military rule. National income from oil had dropped considerably and by 1989, Nigeria's national debt had increased to about $30.5 billion. According to *Debt: A Crisis of Development* published by the United Nations, it was reported that:

> in 1971, the United Nations identified 24 countries as 'least developed' based on their particularly low levels of per capita income and their highly fragile economies. Not one has since climbed out of the category. Rather, more and more have fallen into it...and the 1980s another twelve, bringing the total by the end of 1988 to 42 (p. 2).

There can be no doubt that when the United Nations issued the above statement, it might have included Nigeria due to the perfect match between its description and the state of Nigeria's economy to date. This anemic economy, more than anything else, as expressed in the low social and living standards in the country, reflected the heights of mismanagement of resources which were abundantly available in the 1980s. Some of the mismanagement and waste were widely viewed as politically motivated, encouraged by the pervasive de facto tribal separatism.

It is noteworthy that in Nigeria, the overall political, economic and social bankruptcy [national instability] of the entire country is the price to pay for satisfying ethnic goals. For example, it is documented that when the free and fair 1993 presidential election was conducted and was "won by multimillionaire Industrialist Moshood K.O. Abiola, a member of the Southern Yoruba...General Babaginda...annulled the result of the election because Mr. Abiola was viewed as a threat to the Muslim Northerners" (Aigbogun 1993, A13). With this political episode in mind, it could be said that the handwriting was on the wall – and that the main culprit of Nigeria's economic and political demise was tribalism. The rejection of Mr. Abiola, a Southern Muslim himself, has raised another interesting question relating to the statuses of Southern and Northern Muslims in Nigeria's presidential politics.

In Nigeria, as well as in other parts of Africa, tribal politics is still the dangerous game that people play. In the 1960s, the late Patrice Lumumba of Congo died fighting against tribal politics in the Congo. Influenced by Nkumah's *Class Struggle in Africa*, he saw tribal politics as being responsible for African underdevelopment and advocated "tribal nationalism" instead. He then drew a distinction between tribes and tribalism. Both Nkrumah and Lumumba had believed that tribe, like nationality, was essentially good in every African society while tribalism, which grew out of colonialism was its destruction. Because of the importance which Nkrumah and Lumumba had placed on the concept of tribes and tribalism in Africa, their line of argument deserves an in–depth follow–up in different pages of this text and through other sources as well.

In the colonial days, tribalism, which is still the brainthrust of today's tribal politics in most African countries, was used to exploit African feudal systems and tribal survival, and as a means of combatting the early growth of the National Liberation Movement in Africa. Today tribal politics stands in the way of national unity in most African countries. Nkrumah also maintained, with much regrets, that in the neo–colonial days, tribalism is exploited by the bourgeois African ruling class to divide the masses. Nigeria can be cited as one of these African countries where the influence of tribe and politics complement each other. Most of Nigeria's political agendas are formulated along tribal lines and innuendo. It seems no one can escape this trap, not even the military.

To the degree that Nigeria is neck–deep in tribal politics, its national integration is rendered almost impossible. Historically, Gen. Ironsi who was at first praised for overthrowing the first batch of politicians was later "seen by some as bent on serving the interest of a particular section of Nigeria" (National Youth Service Corps 1973, 90). In this regard, the Decree No. 34 of 1966 which related to the Unitary Republic concept was perceived as a sectional policy by the Northern people at the time when the economic and educational attainment were seemingly unbalanced between the South and the North. It should be remembered that since Lugard's infamous amalgamation of the Southern and Northern protectorates into one Nigeria in 1914, the problem of the so–called social inequality has affected every major political decision made by Nigerian leaders, military and civilian alike.

Howard (1986) studied the activities of the military in Nigeria and observed that "militaries will also intervene as representatives of civilian ruling class factions. Thus the first (Ironsi's) coup in Nigeria in 1966 was perceived to represent the minority Igbo, while the second (Gowon) countercoup was perceived to represent the dominant Northerners" (p. 53). In most recent years, military sectionalism in Nigeria, backed by a civilian ruling class of the same tribe, is slowly becoming a common practice since power can only be retained by force of arms. Additionally, the Nigerian military by utilizing the law of the gun has become almost a permanent replacement of the civilian partisan politics.

In general, politics in Nigeria between the civilian and the military is the story of George Orwell's *Animal Farm* retold whereby Mr. Jones was ousted from the farm because some animals thought of him as totalitarian, elitist and corrupt. The irony is that those animals who led the so-called revolution and ousted Mr. Jones from power soon became more totalitarian, elitist and corrupt than Mr. Jones after they took power. Their slogan that "all animals are equal but some animals are more equal that others" (Orwell 1946, 123) was the testimony of a classed society created and enjoyed by some animals. In practical terms, it appears the Nigerian military, which is pretty much sectional in its leadership composition wants to afford itself a chance of "enjoying power" before the civilian can get to it – a mentality which is based more on a selfish motive than on nationalism. Both the military and civilian politicians encouraged a two-tier economic system of the very rich and the very poor which is seen as responsible for Nigeria's overall political instability and economic underdevelopment.

Worse still, the Nigerian military has been accused of committing or failing to stop the cardinal sins relating to tribalism, elitism and greed. Today, the military is not only perceived as associated with social evils, they are also seen as the agent of tribal totalitarianism in the Nigerian political system. This assessment, as regrettable as it is, is validated by the military's ranks, character and the selection of its leadership since Gowon and the Civil War (see page 137). Since then, the function of the military has changed from that of defending the country to that of ruling the country. We hope to make this point clearer when we discuss the problem of Nigeria's revenue allocation and moral leadership later on. A good example of a moral leader is the late president of the United States, John F. Kennedy. When President John F. Kennedy said to the American people, "Ask not what your country can do for you, ask what you can do for your country," his statement connoted the mark of a moral leader who had the interest of his country at heart. President Kennedy lived his statement and is remembered among other things for his leadership role in America's space program and for being the first president in the U.S. to give up his salary to the country as a gesture of goodwill.

The national interest of Nigeria can be better served if the role of the military is redefined, limiting it to defending the country from outside attacks and maintaining absolute neutrality in partisan politics since their political leadership thus far can not be described as totally exemplary.

On hind–sight, the military rule can be interpreted as preventing their civilian counterpart from learning the art of managing a democratic government. Strict guidelines [division of labor] for the military, police and the civilian politicians in the overall working of the Nigerian society can avert chaos and disjointed government functions. Since independence, the military's function which suddenly took a different dimension has led to an epoc of misrule in Nigeria. Initially, Gen. Gowon professed to prevent Nigeria from disintegration but in October 1970, Gowon declared that "the military leadership would require at least six more years in power..." (McCaskie 1994,653). Since then, it seems anyone who gets into power through the military ranks wants it for life. The concentration is usually not how to relinquish power once it is taken but how to retain it. Gen. Olusegun Obasanjo, a Yoruba who assumed power following Gen. Murtala Muhammed's assassination and peacefully returned the country to the civilian rule, was a rare exception.

Nigeria can help itself by producing leaders with vision in their pursuit of national goals for the common good. In the wake of a changing and competitive world, Nigeria needs leaders who have long range and effective goals to help the country in its political stabilization efforts instead of leaders who engage in the immediate gratification of wealth consumption and cater for tribal interest. Today, it seems that the noted caliber of leaders is in high demand but in short supply, particularly in Africa. Without solving the leadership problem, a country like Nigeria may never be aberrated from the overall darkness of poverty and social evils that surround it.

It is generally believed that while good laws contribute to good government, it is good men and women who make good laws for the society to work. Good men and women in government can be defined as those who uphold high moral integrity since most people will govern and make laws in accordance with their internalized world. A kleptomaniac, for example, would make laws with loopholes so that he can steal while a tribalistic person is apt to make laws favoring his own people only. A fair national government would make laws that do not favor persons or tribes but laws that uphold the country's interest as a whole. The difference between good national leaders and bad ones lie between those who make good national policies and follow them and those who only put up a front to cover for selfish or tribal interests.

To make a case of Nigeria's disintegration at a psychological level, one needs to examine the lyrics of the Nigerian national anthems (old and new) to determine their content validity vis–a–vis tribalism and ethnic discontent. These national anthems are usually recited on special national occasions, cultural events, in schools and universities by youth as a symbol of their national solidarity and loyalty. When Nigerians recite these anthems, the significance of their recitations may be regarded only as a portrayal of hypocrisy of saying something that people do not believe in or have difficulties adopting appropriate behavioral changes based on its implicit truth. Tribal prejudices in Nigeria must be brought to a halt. This argument is based on lack of tribal harmony in the Nigerian society just as we speak. The proof of the hypocrisy is deducible. For example, at the early stage of Nigeria's nationhood when Nigerians were still singing "though tongues and tribes may differ, in brotherhood we stand," tribal mistrust which coated it was running rampant, leading to the bloody civil war.

As a consequence of the diverse "tongues and tribes" in Nigeria, it is increasingly visible that Nigerians are unable to see themselves as being "in brotherhood we stand" in their political decisions and in the sharing of the national cake. The new national anthem ends with "freedom, Peace and Unity." The point is that Nigeria is yet to experience freedom, peace and unity. The word *compatriot* may be regarded as unapplicable to Nigerians as well. This very important observation also seems to support the argument that "but for the intervention of Britain, there would have been no Nigeria and that even as of now, Nigeria remains a mere geographical expression" (National Youth Service Corps 1973, 33). Other contemporary writers have also found a direct link between the current malady in Nigeria and its early foreign invasion and occupation. Goliber (1989, 32) stated that "Nigeria is an outstanding example of a nation created by colonial accident rather than historical evolution. The country has at least 250 different tribal groups..."

These contrasting views of Nigeria's inability to solve its own problems and the harm done by foreign intervention are often times difficult to reconcile. But it is also mind–bothering in trying to imagine what Nigeria could have become without its invasion and occupation by foreigners. Such an imagination can be filled with perhaps wild

NIGERIA: NATIONAL ANTHEMS AND PLEDGE
(excerpts)

1.   New National Anthem:

> Arise O! compatriot,
> Nigeria's call obey
> To serve our fatherland with love and strength and
> faith, the labours of our heroes past shall never be in
> vain. To serve with all our mind one nation bound in
> freedom Peace and Unity.

New National Pledge:

> I pledge to Nigeria my country, to be faithful, loyal
> and honest, To serve Nigeria with all my strength to
> defend our unity and uphold our honour and Glory,
> So help me God. Amen.

2.   Old National Anthem:

> Nigeria we hail thee our own dear Native Land.
> Though tribe and tongue may differ, In brotherhood
> we stand Nigeria's all, and proud to serve our
> sovereign motherland.

Source: *Current Affairs: Nigeria's 30 states and 589 councils.*
Joseph Esu Paul, P.O. Box 1002, Makurdi, Benue State, Nigeria,
JEP Group of Publishers and Advertisers Limited.

speculations if not wishful thinking. National Youth Service Corps (1973), has however maintained that:

> If Africa had been left alone to decide her own political future, and fortune at some stage, an empire could have emerged powerful enough to annex all or most of other minor 'kingdoms' establishing an effective government over territories covering an area, perhaps larger than the size of the present west Africa... (p. 33).

This statement seems to imply that without such an early meddling, Nigeria could have been able to develop its own inertia at its own pace to become self sufficient and integrated.

Nations which had never been colonized and therefore their cultures unadulterated present a case in point. Most people have viewed the recent triumph in the Japanese economy as relating to their abilities to utilize their unadulterated primordial intelligence to develop themselves from "below." On the otherhand, other countries with colonialization experience have been known to make good their independence by seeking to be socially, politically and economically self reliant. Other views relating to Nigerian problems are those brilliantly presented by Yoweri Museveni of Uganda. In his interview with Keith B. Richburg of *The Washington Post* entitled, *Asia and Africa: The Roots of Success and Despair*, he cited the problems of the Africans inter alia as relating to ineffective indigenous leadership, lack of personal discipline, greed, national disintegration and a "widespread corruption of the African ruling elite" (Richburg 1992, A26).

Museveni's statement which reiterated the importance of democracy and economic development, also described the disparity in social and economic development between Asian and African Countries. In the past, Asia and Africa were viewed as possessing essentially the same economic potentials and background. But a recent investigation has revealed that between 1984 and 1990 there existed income and economic growth disparities between the two regions. Based on the comparative per capita income between West Africa and East Asia, it can be assumed that living standards in East Asia is collectively higher than that in West Africa. Whether any generalization can be made for the entire continent of Asia and Africa needs further investigation. But one mystery about Africa is that since 1922 – the year the first African nation obtained it independence – its development has been either very slow, stagnated or deteriorated. For Nigeria in particular, this observation is contrary to the expectation of most economists and political scientists who had earlier proclaimed it as the Giant of Africa. In reviewing the current social, political and economic conditions in Africa as a whole, Mazrui (1986, 11) wrote:

> The ancestors of Africa are angry. For those who believe in the power of ancestors, the proof of their anger is all around us. For those who do not believe in ancestors, the proof of their anger is given another name. . . But what is the proof of the curse of the ancestors? Things are not working in Africa. . .

While almost everybody seems to watch Africa in decay, nobody seems to fully understand the reason(s) behind it. To obtain remedies to Africa's problems, there must be an ongoing study of Africa to compare it to other continents with respect to their political stability, demographic characteristics, and economic data to deduce the disparities in living standards.

As shown in the charts below, Africa qualifies comparatively as a disadvantaged region. Many people have insisted that socio–political and economic stagnation in Africa today is due to the fact that it was colonized. The issue of colonization and its implication on African idealism as well as the effect of ethnic diversity on African instability is significant. For example, Asian countries seem to be more culturally homogenous than their African counterparts. Because they are less diverse culturally, they can put their political houses in order either democratically or dictatorially with less difficulty to enhance their social and economic prosperity. But culture diversity should not be an impediment to social and economic prosperity in society. Rather, its benefits should be utilized in addition to pursuing conditions for liberation such as proper human resource management, strong national leadership, education, nationalism, political and social morality, and an even development predicated by social and economic opportunities for all.

Africa as a whole must decide its proper economic and political destiny. There is a clear choice to be made between politico–economic development and the prevailing underdevelopment. Gans (1992) stated that:

> while there are continuing scholarly and ideological debates about the interplay of different economic, social, cultural and psychological factors that contribute to keeping people poor,

WEST AFRICA AND EAST ASIA:
PER CAPITA INCOME COMPARISON IN U.S. $ 1984–1990

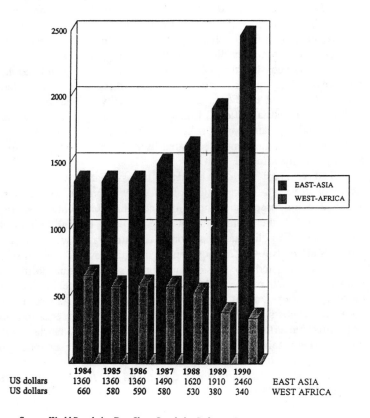

	1984	1985	1986	1987	1988	1989	1990	
US dollars	1360	1360	1360	1490	1620	1910	2460	EAST ASIA
US dollars	660	580	590	580	530	380	340	WEST AFRICA

Source: World Population Data Sheet, Population Reference Bureau, Inc., Washington, DC

consensus is fairly widespread that only when the poor lose the
struggle to escape poverty do they give up mainstream behavior
(A56).

Hubert J. Gans illustrated his viewpoint by resurrecting the concept
of the 'Culture of poverty' which was developed by an anthropologist,
Oscar Lewis, in the 1950s, to describe certain human conditions in
society. The concept suggested that poor people "belonged to a special
culture, passed on from generation to generation, that adapted them so
well to poverty that they did not even want to try to escape it" (p. A56).
Gans maintained that the culture of poverty is closely related to the
concept of "the underclass" – a concept which was propounded by
Gunner Myrdal in 1962 to describe economically displaced people as a
result of industrialization. But abjectness in people such as is
experienced in many parts of Africa takes different forms and comes
from different angles, and is tolerated by its leaders as standard so long
as they are not affected by it.

Today, Third worldism tends to be associated with the vicious
circle of poverty – a condition of underdevelopment which is self–
afflicted or imposed by outside influence. In a pluralistic society the
availability of the conditions of liberation is crucially important.
Unfortunately, in Nigeria, these conditions are somehow in a declining
mode. Most Advocates for social and economic development in society
have also indicated an erosion in Nigeria's education, politics and
economy as each military dictatorship continues to be ineffective in
tackling the root cause of Nigeria's underdevelopment. As a result, most
political scientists are forced to speculate Nigeria's disintegration given
its political uncertainty of the moment. The fact is that Nigeria has deep
rooted and unresolved psychosocial issues on which such an apocalyptic
disintegration is based.

In an article entitled: *North Can Stand On Its Own*, the Former
Senator Kanti Bello from Katsina is quoted as saying:

> . . .North has been unjustifiably maligned as drawing back Nigeria's
> progress – Hausa–Falani man was better off in the days of the late
> Saduana of Sokoto – fed up with people especially Southern Press
> ascribing the nation's problems to Hausa–Falani. The people of the
> North where I come from want their dignity." (Usigbe, 1994, p. 1)

Bello's statement was suggestive though not conclusive of an
impending national disintegration – an attempt to turn back the hands

of Nigeria's national clock, from nationalism to strong regionalism and tribal consciousness.

Essentially between mid 1950s and mid 1990s there existed two types of leadership in Nigeria. The first type of leadership emerged before the Nigerian independence in 1960, characterized by blind nationalism for nationhood without much thoughts on how the nation would be run. To most Nigerians of that era, independence from Britain symbolized a lifetime achievement – an end in itself. The second type of leadership emerged after independence, characterized by blind tribalism for tribal affiliation in which the concept of nationhood seemed secondary. This period also marked the beginning of the emergent corruption and greed. In all of this, the one unanswered question is still how the regression from a deep sense of nationalism to no sense of nationalism occurred – how nationalism was replaced by tribalism.

In spite of the numerous constitutional conferences, the military coup d'etat and the lip service toward national integration, the psychosocial problems of ethnicity in Nigeria have never been taken up in good faith by any Nigerian leader in our recent memory for fear of tribal alienation. While other countries are confronting issues of multiethnicity forthrightly within the framework of a central government, Nigerian leaders have tiptoed around Nigeria's core problem for 33 years. By so doing, they have successfully promoted its political instability and underdevelopment as well. Geopolitically, Nigeria may be losing ground since most multinational investments thrive under the condition of political stability by host countries. Specifically to Nigeria, and Africa in general, the above statement may be a moot point since it is usually a selected few in these societies who normally stand to benefit more from any choatic political situation; the masses get the chaff. Some Nigerians, including the military, tend to thrive on sentimentalizing tribalism, elitism and greed. Overall, for a country to develop socially and economically, the key is having a stable democratic government. The main problem of Nigeria is centered around political instability by design, lack of unity among its many tribes and the national leadership which seems to be out of touch with the nation's social and economic realities.

Leadership for bread and not for guns...

Chapter Two

Ethnicity and Related Theories

Behavioral theorists have been in the forefront of finding the causes of human conflict under such headings as ethnic aggression, violence, domination, prejudices, power and values, to name a few. Throughout history, human beings have been known to be in conflict with one another based on ethnicity.

Ethnic–conflict in Africa [Nigeria] is the latest chronicle among a series of such conflicts in time and place. The Genesis account of the Bible describes the conflict between the children of Adam and Eve in which Cain killed Abel as the oldest kindred conflict known to man. Similarly, the conflict between the present day Israelis and Arabs generally known as the Middle East Conflict tend to follow the same pattern. Historically, the Israelites and the Arabs are known to be the respective descendant children of Isaac and Ishmael whose father was Abraham. It is recorded that from childhood the seeds of Abraham namely Isaac and Ishmael hated each other and have been in constant conflict since then. Even though it seems inconceivable that blood relatives should behave in the manner thus described, many social scientists have investigated the causes of human conflict in general.

Accordingly, many of the human conflicts can be traced to the concept of human survival. The Darwinian theory, as contained in the Origin of Species (1859) saw this behavior as basic to all human beings. Belief in the "survival of the fittest" may be interpreted as the struggle for scarce human needs to the extent that human confrontation becomes inevitable. In this struggle, Darwin maintains that it is the very fit that will survive over the very weak. The idea of self-preservation in the absence of morality or ethical consideration therefore underlies the basic interpretation of the Darwinian theory. The other interpretation implied in Darwinian theory is that some organisms are naturally "fitter" than the others to survive their harsh environmental conditions or are better able to adapt to their natural habitat. Natural fitness in the later sense can be interpreted to mean physical and intellectual abilities to change the odds. Either of these interpretations seems aptly applicable to human beings as they continue to interface with one another in their environment in search for need fulfillment. What are human needs? Abraham Maslow in 1955 theorized basic human needs, hierarchically ranging from physiological needs to safety, belongingness/love, esteem and finally to self-actualization needs.

Before we proceed further, one point that is crucial with regards to need fulfillment must be mentioned. Every individual in society must continue to hanker for need fulfillment. But if a society denies its citizen opportunities to strive for basic need fulfillment, it is indeed cultivating an impoverished society of continuous circle of poverty. Children, for instance need nutritious food, love, a warm and accepting environment, and freedom from fear and so on to grow and become productive members of society. Adults, in much the same way, need an environment of peaceful coexistence with their neighbors in order to be productive in their daily lives. "Peaceful coexistence" implies the ability to fulfill the need for belongingness and acceptance by others while esteem and actualization needs imply abilities to legitimately fulfill the need for self confidence, power, prestige and status and to be all one can be in a society. Above all, human environment must continue to be conducive for economic investment through which basic physiological needs – education, legal protection, jobs, property ownership, and security from bodily and mental harm are provided.

Human reaction to unfulfilled needs is universal. Therefore, the old adage that a hungry man is an angry man is an expression of an unfulfilled need for physiological, safety, love, esteem and self-actualization needs. For example, a Yoruba man, a Hausa man would be as equally disturbed as an Igboman or an Ibibioman if any of his basic needs are denied or withheld. A person whose needs are denied or withheld, or who is fearful that they are going to be denied or withheld may exhibit a violent or prejudicial behavior for self

HUMAN NEEDS

Source: Maslow's Hierarchy of Need
Adapted from Maslow, 1954

protection. They may become mentally depressed or physiologically ill. They may then behave irrationally towards other people. One final point associated with need dissatisfaction is that it relates to creative thinking deficits. This point becomes crucial since the ability to think creatively tends to correlate with developmental levels either in individuals or in society. A well developed individual is likely to be more efficient and creative in the work place than a less developed individual. The same principle can be extended to the entire society. We feel that unless people can liberate themselves from the stagnation of basic need dissatisfaction, they cannot embark on what Maslow called "growth motivation" to achieve developmental goals.

In history, marginalized or oppressed people have been known to exhibit behavior which Rogers (1959) called the actualizing tendency i.e. "inherent tendency of the organism to develop all its capacities in ways which serve to maintain or enhance the organism" (p. 16). These tendencies are basic in all human beings enabling them to meet their fundamental needs. Whenever an effort to achieve need fulfillment is thwarted, the result is human frustration. It is this sense of abjectness which has caused much civil unrest in many societies and amongst groups of people who are racially or ethnically divided and may be afraid of social, economic or physical annihilation.

Today, social unrest and violence in Nigeria have reached an epidemic proportion. A growing body of research has indicated that social unrest, violence and their underlying causes are all rooted in irrational human mind and misdeeds. Common sense has it that they are counterproductive to the overall social good and should be controlled at all cost. Freudian psychology theorized the psychic apparatus to include the id, ego and the superego. Of these three personality representations, the id represents an individual's instinctual, neurotic personality which may be linked to violence, social unrest and desire for social domination to satisfy a need. Social evils, though prevalent in our societies today, are not unstoppable events. There is need however, for an individual [leader] to develop his inner tendencies that are helpful in dealing adequately with irrational behavior and in defeating or at least maintaining a balance with self–defeating urges of the Id – urges relating to hate, cheating, corruption, bribery, fighting, tribalism, abuse of power and immorality. Understanding the interaction of the psychic apparatus has been widely recommended by most social scientists as a prelude to understanding basic human behavior. Coleman (1972) explained the interaction of the psychic apparatus when he stated that:

Ego develops and mediates between the demands of the id and the realities of the external world. Since the id–ego relationship is merely one of expediency, Freud introduced the third key subsystem ––the superego––which is the outgrowth of learning the taboos and moral values of society. The superego is essentially what we refer to as conscience, and is concerned with right and wrong. As the superego develops, we find an additional inner control system coming into operation to cope with the uninhibited desires of the id (p. 53).

B.F. Skinner experimented on rats to deduce human reaction to environmental factors. Much of his research outcomes have found relevance in teaching and learning, human development and human motivation. The basic thrust of Skinner Operant Conditioning therefore seems to imply that human beings will learn and repeat behaviors that are meaningful to them since what we now know as culture is learned. Heavy emphasis is rather placed on the instrumentation, meaning that the response received from human endeavors will depend on the methods of human stimulation for and reinforcement of a desired behavior. It is at this juncture that teachers, parents, church leaders and politicians can play an important role in shaping their societies.

Theory Z by William Ouchi sheds more light on the importance of an enriched environment and human empathy to enhance quality of life and social harmony. Douglas McGregor presents two divergent representations of the social man namely, the Theory X and Theory Y. Theory X usually paints the picture of the lazy and unmotivated man – the drone of the society– while Theory Y is represented by the productive and self–motivated individual who works hard towards personal growth and that of his society. In spite of these representations, the burden still resides on those in society with the responsibility of improving the overall environment for all who live in it. We will belabor this point by saying that both Theory X and Theory Y characters are inherent in each and every individual, ie. he can be motivated or unmotivated. Those in authority by their actions must determine what personalities or behaviors they intend to bring out of or mould from their followers. Lau (1975) though writing from the private industry perspective rather than from a public policy standpoint, suggested how the entire human ecology can be managed to achieve human needs. He stated that:

Most major theorists such as Maslow, McGregor, Herzberg, and McClelland stress the importance of creating the conditions in which the individual can fulfill his own needs in the process of achieving organizational goals. . . (Lau, 1975, 51)

Other pertinent works dealing with learning behavior, human development and environmental adaptation include those advocated by theorists like Thorndike, Pavlov, Kohler, Weitheimer and mostly John B. Watson, who "emphasized the importance of environmental influence on development as opposed to hereditary factors" (Smith and Smith 1958, 25). Watson's research conclusion was not only a scientific affidavit toward an inclusive society but also a nullification of Author Jensen's study which was pregnated with racism in explaining lower IQ (Intelligence Quotient) scores for Blacks as compared to Whites in the United States. Jensen's study was disavowed worldwide not only for lack of scientific credibility but also for its racial overtone designed to brand Blacks as unteachable. Marden and Meyer (1978) regarded the study as a "biological fallacy" stating that:

Author Jensen, a contemporary American, is the chief exponent of the primacy of genetic difference in an explanation of lower IQ scores for Blacks as compared to Whites. Jensen has used a wide comparative data but in the first place his use of the genetic factor is simplistic. (p. 90)

By and large, social harmony is based on creating an enriched environment for all who live and work in a given society. Culturally diverse groups of people can coexist in harmony if the society is properly managed. Leaders of all walks of life should concern themselves with being gestalt centered, by developing the "whole" society instead of parts of the society which are most beneficial to them. Gestalt's interest in the integration of all parts is inherent in forging ethnic and racial harmony and peaceful coexistence among diverse peoples. When a pluralistic society is integrated through an even distribution of national wealth and social amenities, citizens will learn to coexist in peace.

POWER AND ETHNICITY

In most multiethnic societies, the importance of power and power struggle cannot be overlooked. Power struggle in almost all situations has its economic, social, as well as ethical implications. It is a natural human instinct having its roots in the desire to escape deprivation, domination, oppression, physical and mental pain. Power struggle can also be seen as seeking a vantage position in the social stratum. Wrightsman (1972,73) stated that ". . . all social behavior is a direct or disguised reflection of power seeking." Wrightsman tended to describe power seeking as obsessive, compulsive and brutal and devoid of the virtues of the "alleged motives of altruism, love, truth and religion" (p. 73). The implied classification and segregation of individuals in society into subgroups such as the powerful and the powerless is widely documented. Jung (1978,126) wrote:

> From what we have asserted about the destructive nature of powerlessness, one might conclude that powerfulness was the panacea and that those with power would be free to be creative, human and fulfilled. Although this potential may exist, power does not automatically bestow those blessings on its holders. As the old cliche' goes, power corrupts, often bringing out the worst in terms of arrogance and snobbery.

The desire for power and prestige in all its ramifications can be cited as one of the reasons for most inter–ethnic conflicts. But we must separate achievement needs from the desire for power and prestige as is commonly employed in the third world. Wrightsman (1972, 125) defined "achievement motive as an energizing condition that causes a person to internalize evaluation of his own performance and then seek to meet these standards." Anderson and Faust (1973) believed that achievement is a concern for achieving success and avoiding failure. Whenever a person achieves success, he is happy, respected and applauded by others. For a leader to be respected and applauded, his achievement must reflect followers' achievements and vice versa.

Historically, names that can be associated with achievement for the common good as opposed to power seeking for selfish ends are included in the short list below to exemplify who we can call men with "humanitarian ambition." They are Charles de Gaule in the Fifth Republic of France, Nelson Mandela in apartheid South Africa, Abraham Lincoln of the United States for freeing the slaves and saving the Union, and Martin Luther King, Jr. in non–violent struggle for freedom. To add to the list are African leaders such as Patrice Lumumba, Kwame Nkrumah, Franz Fanon, and Leopold Sedar Senghor who had devoted their lives to liberating Africa from colonialism. We cannot however, forget leaders like Dr. Nnamdi Azikiwe, Chief Obafami Awolowo, Sir Abubakar Tafewa Belewa and Chief Udo Udoma for their pioneering roles in obtaining Nigerian independence from Britain –a task which in our opinion, has represented the only real achievement not smothered by ethnic division, prejudice and power mongering. According to Sheikh Batu Daramy these early African leaders provided a "useful background material of the thoughts, feelings, suffering of colonial peoples and the aspirations of Africans and persons in the African diaspora" (Daramy 1983,32).

In an ethnocentric sense, to be powerful is a need which most individuals or groups of individuals in society must satisfy to stay on top. To them, it represents a life fulfillment with its aims usually directed toward the grand economic gains in the social structure. Take, for example, an individual whose financial and political power have been met, may exhibit the behavior of perceiving the powerless as unmotivated and worthless. He is concerned with enriching himself and influencing others. Alternatively, he can bring about social change and help others by putting the people whom he serves first. As it was pointed out earlier, "power corrupts power." Hence most contemporary social scientists have found the need to focus on ethical standards governing the use of power in society, defining what the proper ethical behavior and conduct of the powerful should be, and generally emphasizing the power of the majority in a democratic process.

Each nation, is expected to have its rules and regulations to curb an abuse of power. But such domestic rules and regulations have been overshadowed by the interpretation of individuals or groups of individuals who rely on their opinion regarding what constitutes an abuse of power. International organizations such as the United Nations (UN), Organization for African Unity (OAU), Organization of Arab States (OAS), and so on, are acting as watchdogs to prevent abuse of power and violation of human rights. International military organizations such as the United Nations Emergency Force (UNEF) and the Military Observer Group (ECOMOG) of the Economic Community of the West African States (ECOWAS) have performed such roles as supervise armistices and maintain economic sanctions under the direction of their parent organizations.

But in recent years, there has been some misgivings concerning the effectiveness of these regional and world bodies. They have not been able to stop most of the internal power struggles and internecine warfare in Africa and elsewhere. As Howard (1986) indicated the OAU's ability to protect the rights of individual Africans was almost non-existent. Its function, in addition to the "protection of rights of heads of states, . . . appears to be to hold enormously expensive annual meetings, sometimes costing a considerable proportion of the host country's budget" (p. 4). It seems obvious that an organization such as the OAU should by now recognize ethnic power struggle as the cause of instability in most African countries and live up to its charter of protecting human rights abuses by the powerful in countries like Nigeria, Zaire, Somalia, Ethiopia, Rwanda and Liberia to name a few.

While the above countries have experienced full blown factional fighting in recent years, there are other countries like South Africa, Nigeria, Ghana, Serria Leone and so on where factional fighting is in the making. Examples of different African political systems are given in Africa Démos, classified into seven broad areas: Democratic, Authoritarian, strong commitment to democracy, moderate commitment to democracy, ambiguous commitment to democracy, directed democracy and contested sovereignty " (see Africa Démos, 1994,27). According to this document, there tends to be no strong commitment to democracy anywhere in Africa. Overall, most African democracies so far are fragile. "Nigeria" is listed as having an authoritarian system of government alongside with Libya and sudan. An authoritarian system of government is defined as:

> a system with highly restricted opportunities for political mobilization. Power is exercised by a leader or small group of leaders who are not formally accountable to the electorate. There are no effective constitutional limits to the exercise of power. (Africa Démos 1994,27)

Authoritarianism is linked to power seeking. Hilgard (1953, 156) stated that "the desire for prestige and the desire for power are related. Prestige is the desire for recognition and acclaim; the desire for power is the desire for influence for response by others to oneself as an agent." In some societies, most especially in the Third World, power and prestige needs are usually satisfied at the expense of the lower class.

POLITICAL SYSTEM IN AFRICA

COUNTRIES	TYPE OF POLITICAL SYSTEM
Algeria	Contested Sovereignty
Egypt	Directed Democracy
Libya	Authoritarian
Morocco	Directed Democracy
Sudan	Authoritarian
Tunisia	Moderate Democracy
Western Sahara	Contested Sovereignty
Benin	Democratic
Burkina Faso	Moderate Democracy
Cape Verde	Democratic
Cote D'lvoire	Moderate Democracy
Gambia	Contested Sovereignty
Ghana	Moderate Democracy
Guinea	Ambiguous Democracy
Guinea Bissau	Moderate Democracy
Liberia	Contested Sovereignty
Mali	Democratic
Mauritana	Moderate Democracy
Niger	Democratic
Nigeria	Authoritarian
Senegal	Democratic
Sierra leone	Moderate Democracy
Togo	Ambiguous
Burundi	Contested Sovereignty
Comoros	-----
Djibouti	Moderate Democracy
Ethiopia	Moderate Democracy
Kenya	Moderate Democracy
Madagascar	Democratic
Malawi	Democratic
Mauritius	Democratic
Mozambique	Moderate Democracy
Reunion	-----

POLITICAL SYSTEM IN AFRICA continued

COUNTRIES	TYPE OF POLITICAL SYSTEM
Rwanda	Contested Sovereignty
Seychelles	Moderate Democracy
Somalia	Contested Sovereignty
Tanzania	Moderate Democracy
Uganda	Moderate Democracy
Zambia	Democratic
Zimbabwe	Moderate Democracy
Angola	Contested Sovereignty
Cameroon	Directed Democracy
Central African	Democratic
Republic	Ambiguous Democracy
Chad	Democratic
Congo	Ambiguous Democracy
Equitorial Guinea	Moderate Democracy
Gabon	Democratic
Sao Tome and	
Principe	Ambiguous Democracy
Zaire	Democratic
Botswana	Ambiguous Democracy
Lesotho	Democratic
Nambia	Democratic
South Africa	Ambiguous Democracy
Swaziland	Moderate Democracy
Eritrea	Moderate Democracy

Source: Adapted from Africa Démos, *Africa 1994: Ecstasy and Agony*. A Bulleting of the African Governance Program – The Carter Center, September 1994, vol. III, Number 3,p.27.

The exercise of influence and dominance of one group over another—and the establishment of authoritarian administration is expressed in the Machiavellian Doctrine (1469 – 1527) --a doctrine which believes that those in authority should rule by fear and not by love and that power is the preferable means by which leaders should lead. This doctrine is becoming more ingrained in Africa, more so than any other part of the world, not even in Europe where the doctrine was first conceived. Howard (1986, 45) stated that in Africa, "most governments are dominated by the military, by a one–party bureaucracy or by a no–party dictatorship." Because this form of government is inconsistent with the 20th century partisan politics it has caused social instability and economic underdevelopment in Africa.

In Nigeria, for example, hanging on to power no matter whose "ox is tied" has been a common practice since the Civil War. There is need to understand why most Nigerians as well as other African leaders like to remain in power in spite of their poor leadership performances. We see three main reasons for the behavior:

1. Personal greed, arrogance and innate individual desire to satisfy the need for power.
2. Tribalistic and selfish tendencies on the part of the power holder to retain power as a mandate for his own tribe and as a means of controlling natural resources.
3. The syndrom of the pre–colonial and colonial years when kings and their henchmen ruled with absolute authority; and since the mentality has not been eradicated, it is easy for those who hold power to transferentially treat their nations as their kingdoms or colonies.

The Washington Times report of August 7, 1993 captioning: a Nigerian Moves to Retain Power revealed how "Nigeria's ruler unveiled another maneuver . . . to try to hang onto power –a move criticized by opponents as an attempt to transform military ruler to civilian leader" (A.9). This statement was made in reference to the precedented attempt of the ex–military leader, Ibrahim Babaginda, to hold on to power –a position he had held for about eight years, and now held by Sani Abacha who for eight years was "General Babaginda's right hand man" (Newswatch, 1994, 10). As Babaginda had done, "Abacha pledged to return to civilian rule, although he has given no date for his departure. Instead, he has called for a four month long constitutional conference to begin June 27" (Shiner, 1994, A27). It should be borne in mind that in most African countries like Nigeria where there is no clearcut ethnic majority, the difficulty of establishing a singular ethnic powerbase is usually enormous. In these countries, politico–economic powerbase is established either through ethnic coalition, by force of arms or by having a grip on natural resources. To this end, Nigeria's military has progressed from executing a series of bloody coup d'etat to bloodless ones. But in other African countries where bloodless coups are unknown, ethnic struggle for power has remained enduring, brutal and egoistic. Hence, most of the internecine wars in Black Africa have been nothing but gruesome. The Rwandan, Ethiopian, Somalian and the Liberian and certainly the Nigerian–Biafrian (1967–1972) Wars are immediate examples. Like hell–fire igniting from nowhere, the built–in hatred of one tribe or ethnic group against another would lead to an impudent killing of one tribe by another.

What seems to bother those outside these borders of violence is how people who have lived together for years, perhaps shared the same ancestry, drunk from the same stream and shared common borders and sometimes intermarried, can all of a sudden start killing one another with guns, knives, spears and machetes.   Reporting on Rwanda (Richburg 1994, A1) gave an example as well as the nature of an African tribal conflict by stating that:

> Although details were sketchy the violence suggested a breakdown of a truce reached last year between Rwanda's government dominated by members of the majority Hintu tribe, and a three year–old rebel movement of minority Tutsis. Clashes between the two tribes have flared periodically in both Rwanda and Burundi and caused tens of thousands of deaths since the nation gained independence from Belgium in 1962.

Thomas Hobbes (1588 – 1679) maintained that human conditions could be viewed as a "war of all against all" and that man's main preoccupation is power. Similarly, Nietzsche (1844 – 1900) believed that power was the most endearing motive of man and that his goals should be different from "goals prescribed by traditional ethical religious systems" (Morse, 1970, 6540). In African tribal politics, the above statements are sometimes taken quite literally.

Accordingly, in most Third World countries such as Nigeria where politics is rooted in ethnicity, the belief in brute force to obtain political power is even stronger. Political parties for power gains are usually formed along ethnic lines. Howard (1986, 137) stated that:

> the problem in Nigerian politics is that separate regional power groups manipulate ethnic sentiments to acquire political and economic resources. In the Nigerian system of patron–client politics, all patron groups must be accommodated; otherwise, even though the threat of regional schism was removed by the federal victory in 1967–70 Civil War, the possibility remains that regional elites will manipulate contacts within the military to forment coup d'etat."

The fact is that no galvanizing national interests stronger than tribal interest have ever been developed in Nigeria. Therefore, in order to have a dominative political majority to govern, Nigerian politics usually ends up in one of the following two ways: 1) politics of ethnic conflicts and 2) politics of ethnic coalition neither of which had produced any useful political result in the past. A dominative group ethnocentrically speaking is defined as "one that shares a common history, common value system, a common language and that is able to control sufficient economic and political power to protect and advance its own group interest over that of other groups" (Marden and Meyer 1978, 21).

Under the prevailing circumstances, Nigerian dictatorships along with the military have mushroomed as an alternative to an unachievable all–civilian ethnic consensus in national partisan politics. In the First Republic of Nigeria (1960–1963) for example, it was the National Council for Nigerian Citizens (NCNC), an eastern based political party which formed a coalition with the Northern Peoples' Congress (NPC), a northern based party in order to achieve the needed political power base – United People Grand Alliance (UPGA). But because of ethnic differences that alliance did not work for too long. Its aftermath was the 1963 bloodshed and the culminating Civil War. During the Civil War, it was apparently obvious that the North alone could not win the war. Hence to tilt the military equation, an ethnic coalition between Northerners, Westerners and a part of Southeasterners was formed against Biafra. It must be borne in mind that there were some people who saw the Nigerian Civil War as a war between the North and East, each accusing the other of attempting ethnic and religious domination. Since then, all attempts for a political democracy have been on a downhill slope.

In 1979, Shagari's National Party of Nigeria (NPN), an all Nigerian civilian government also failed to provide a sustainable political policy towards Nigeria's unity inspite of NPN's multi-ethnic outlook as demanded within the "constitutional provision for National representatives" (Howard, 1986, 137). McCaskie (1994, 655) stated that "by the early 1980s. . .NPN politicians dominated by a powerful political community in Kaduna distributed contracts and rewards in order to ensure their own continuation in power." During his term in office, Shagari was also seen as moving to join forces with Azikiwe's Nigerian People Party (NPP) "to reinforce its power on the federal legislature" (p. 655). David Mark in his April 1994 interview with *Newswatch* implied that the military having seen the opportunity "are spending all this time and energy trying to find how they will retain power. . ." (Newswatch 1994,14).

In all of this, there is something very frightening about the concept of ethnic power struggle in Nigeria's national politics, viewed generally as counterproductive to the economic, social and political well-being of the society. Despite this warning, many of the political and military leaders have thrived in exploiting the weakness of the ethnic diversity for their own personal ambition for power and wealth. There is need to understand the difference between power and achievement needs within the context of leadership in society.

Between 1400s and 1900s, individuals have experienced general attitudinal and behavioral changes which have affected follower-leadership relationship in society. Power as a divine right of the king or of the privileged few was first challenged starting with the position taken by Martin Luther (1483-1546) toward the authority and certain practices of the Catholic Church. Since then, there are recorded incidences in history whereby powerful leaders have been challenged, even deposed by their followers for unethical behavior and unpopularity. Quite a few examples of deposed leaders have existed in recent history including Ferdinand Marcos of the Philippines (1968) and the Shah of Iran (1979).

The distinction between power and authority should be studied and understood by those who intend to use them. Such a distinction is intended to lie in the full understanding of powerholding either as a "divine right" or "trusteeship." It is only when all these concepts are grasped and utilized that democracy can be fully guaranteed. In recent years, we have witnessed examples of the type of changes which are likely to continue to satisfy the need for democracy. The collapse of the Soviet Empire, the 1992 Student's rebellion in China, student's rebellions in Nigeria, Civil Liberty Organization (CLO) and the Community for Democracy (CD) in Nigeria and the dismantling of apartheid in South Africa are all signs of the beginning of the end of political oppression and abuse of power by political and military leaders. It is a human tragedy that in the twentieth century, some nations are still unable to progress from the totalitarianism of Niccoló Machiavelli (1459–1527), to the democracy of the U.S. President – Thomas Jefferson (1743–1826) who advocated self–determination and individual freedom within the context of an elected government.

ETHNIC VALUES AND PREJUDICE

Tribal politics in Nigeria in most cases reflect tribal values. Care must be taken to differentiate African tribal politics from interest politics of the Western World. These two concepts, though closely related in some ways, are different in many other ways. The differences are mostly derived form the value systems of the subcultures. Interest politics is seeking to achieve the minority interest within the framework of a democratic process while tribal politics can be interpreted as seeking to achieve tribal interest by force regardless of national interest.

To discern tribal values multiethnically without discussing its relationships with such concept as the *self* is like trying to row a boat without an oar. Equally associated with tribal values is the culture in which an individual grew up. After a child is born, he is quickly affected rather instinctively by both cultural and biological factors. Biological factors such as eating, toileting, crying and drinking are common and universal to all children while cultural factors such as drive, competitiveness, subordinativeness, cooperativeness, aggressiveness and so on are specific and uncommon to other children outside the relative culture. Hence the basic differences in children tend to lie in the relationship with their culturally significant others. Tribalism is an example of a cultural variable which is learned and transmitted by the leader, formally or informally. Gordon Alport explained behavior differences in people in terms of an individual's trait factors, somehow analogous to cultural factors. A cultural factor is the individual's characteristic that can be observed or measured, and capable of distinguishing one tribal group from the other. This cultural factor can be graduated ranging from most to least pervasive disposition of behavior, explaining why some tribal groups in a society like Nigeria can be more tribalistic than others. Today, there are reported cases of institutionalized tribalism in Nigeria, not only in politics but also in most parastatals and other governmental agencies.

Marden and Meyer (1978, 269) stated that a "culture has historical roots." As individuals cluster in a cultural environment as defined either by their anthropological, sociological, or economic affiliation, they by their heritage begin to develop, maintain and dynamize certain lifestyles, folkways, attitudes and belief systems which are valuable only to them. In Nigeria, as well as other parts of Africa these social factors are always so powerful and relative to the group, that they become the nucleus of existence and for which tribal politics is based. In this sense, a tribal system is like a trap which holds an individual and prevents him from full participation in the events of the larger society.

Most social psychologists would agree that a culture is important in shaping human adaptation to his environment and therefore, has a function in ego formation and development. The ego is sometimes referred to as a differentiated or inferred self. The self, relative to tribal values can be best understood when its appropriate prefixes are attached. It is in this sense that the importance of self–concept, self–esteem, and self–identity in the understanding of human behavior have been widely stressed. Hamacheck (1978, 6) described ego as:

> that portion of personality structure that embodies the core of decision making, planning and defensiveness. . . thus the ego is a construction from behavior, a hypothetical construct that though it can not be directly observed, can be inferred from one's behavior.

Hamacheck's additional statement that the self grows within the social framework tends to imply how group associations such as tribal groups, religious groups, even work groups are apparent in strengthening the ego state. The more group members identify and master group norms, the more they satisfy their individual propelling needs for self identity, self–esteem and self–worth. How a man thinks and behaves thereafter are closely linked to the acculturated value of his subculture. The interrelationship between values, ego and culture is explained by Krech, Crutchfield and Ballachey (1962, 102) when they stated that "values reflect the culture of the society and are widely shared by the members of the culture. If the individual accepts a value for himself, it may become a goal for him." So far, our discussion on values has centered on intracultural behavior of an individual. How an individual behaves interculturally is important as well. Merril (1969, 80) posited that:

> Man is a social and cultural animal and his behavior can be fully grasped on his double context. During his social development in a particular cultural setting, an individual develops a personality that has certain qualities in common with other members of the society as well as certain qualities unique to him.

According to the above statement, a man's intercultural behavior is also essential in understanding his social and economic well–being, the well–being of his subculture as well as that of the larger society. In today's multiethnic societies such as Nigeria, strict cultural relativity is a myth. Because of social and economic interdependence between one man and another, between one culture and another, the cultural membrane between neighbors has become apparently more porous causing them to interface either at peace or war.

Intercultural rivalry underscores the basic nature of man. One of these basic nature is his competitiveness. Others are greed, aggression and dominativeness. There are two types of competitions, namely, fair and unfair. Only fair competition should be encouraged. Fair competition fulfills man's purposefulness in achieving his goal orientation needs. Unfair competition is the relationship between extortions and dishonesty to achieve personal goals. Some of the techniques employed in extortion across cultural lines include self–inflation and value judgment as a starting point, primarily to put one culture over another and to maneuver for positions of advantage.

Tribal prejudice can be seen as a child born out of self–inflation and value judgement expressed in "I am okay, you're not okay." Banks (1979,68) defined prejudice as "a set of rigid and unfavorable attitudes toward a particular group or groups which is formed in disregard to facts." Name calling and dehumanization of others are the two common forms of social prejudice with a lot of psychological implications in humans. Most people often think that other people are less than they, whether they can prove it or not. But we see subcultural superiority as a matter of self–perception which, more often than not is socially erroneous within the overall struggle for an individual's need to be self sufficient. Over the years, most social scientists have found a correlation between prejudice and economic survival. Karl Marx described the traditional belief relating to rulers' exploitation of the laboring class.

Other forms of prejudice are related to economic scarcity or the fear thereof when the working class may discriminate among themselves based on tribal, ethnic or racial backgrounds. It is not surprising that in most societies, including Nigeria, there exist the tendency to search for the scum. In Nigeria there is no scum, contrary to what some tribes would like to believe. Much of what is known of Nigeria today is artificial; from early migration, to colonization, to territorial fission–fusion to indigenous rulership.

From a practical point of view, one should maintain that tribal values in Nigeria are only valuable to the extent that they do not conflict with or take precedence over overall national interest and goal. In Nigeria, as well as other African countries, there is need to develop a national culture of economic, social and political dimensions. This culture ought to be strong enough to galvanize every citizen towards national unity while helping to maintain ethnic individuality and self–identity in the process. Because we live in a society of economic, social and cultural shareability, much of our energy should be directed toward equitable distribution of wealth, cultural exchange and peaceful coexistence with our neighbors.

Chapter Three

Ethnicity in the Global Perspective

Until the early 1960s, very little was known of the danger posed by problems of intra-racial diversity, sometimes referred to as ethnic or tribal diversity. In a country like India, this problem comes in another but similar name – the caste. Much of the global attention was focused on the conflict of racial diversity. The reason for this is simple. First, the notion of tribes or ethnicity was limited to Africa where it was carefully managed through colonial decentralization policies. The system of indirect rule was one way of keeping different segments of society separate and bureaucratic.

While Britain was open about its decentralization policy in Africa, that is, treating the colonial people as second class subjects, the French policy of assimilation was hypocritical and had variations for African colonies. Harris (1987, 187) stated that ". . .the French did not provide the means for achieving assimilation of the African into French society and culture. It should be recognized, however, that most Africans preferred their own culture anyway. . ." For years, while the colonialists were engaging in economic activities, there was little or no meaningful and competitive interface between different ethnic groups of African natives. Colonial separatist policies in Africa were both physical and ideological. Trading which was the colonialists' preoccupation was carried out directly between local businessmen and the representative of a colonial company. Consequently, infrastructure such as roads were built only to enhance the colonialists' commercial interests. Most African roads in the colonial era only connected colonial commercial buildings with different seaports where raw materials were shipped overseas. By promoting disconnectedness among Africans, the colonialists could control ethnic conflict among Africans during the colonial rule by keeping each tribal group separate from the other. The colonial separatist policy of yesterday has however become Africa's problem of today. Such lack of interethnic coexistence was likely to cause tribal alienation. For example, during the colonial rule, Nigerians of different tribal backgrounds seldom had the opportunity to relate [formulate a common goal or had a common purpose] with each other at any close proximity. Minus the transportation problem already discussed there were little or no linkage programs before and after 1914 to connect Nigerian tribal groups emotionally. Student's educated in colonial schools were forced to study the British Empire history or the French Revolution which did not properly orient Nigerians on Nigeria's history, let alone African history. Consequently, Nigerians from the far north of the country were as alien as the colonialists to Nigerians from the far south and vice versa. In general, each tribal chief (*emir, obong, oba, eze*) as authorized by the colonialists had his territory and people to manage. In essence, many Nigerians by living in their separate "Colonialistic" localities – colonies within a colony – had become strangers to one another in their land for many years. An attempt toward ethnic cooperation in Nigeria did not come until much later. By early 1960s, it was quickly learnt that to bring all Nigerians under one organizational umbrella of Federalism was the hardest nut to crack. Since then, the indigenous central government of Nigeria which could have brought Nigerians of different tribes together have lacked the political muscle to achieve this goal.

Elsewhere in the world, the problem of ethnic diversity and conflict were managed differently. The Indian tribes of North America were pretty much contained in their reservations until as late as the 1950s. In the former Soviet Union, ethnic groups were bound together by the mighty forces of Communist totalitarianism. It was only at the collapse of the Soviet empire in the early 1990s that most of the ethnic divisiveness and conflicts such as in Bosnia became problematic. Between the 1930s and 1940s Hitler's "crime against humanity" did not only bring racial hatred in Germany into global view, it spearheaded the second global conflict – the second World War (WWII). At the end of WWII and the defeat of Hitler, racial conflicts were domesticated to the United States and South Africa under the policy of segregation and apartheid, respectively. Meanwhile, the rest of Europe maintained the appearance of being racially tolerant because of its interest in Africa. With the dissipation of racial tension in the U.S. and recently in South Africa, ethnic tensions have captured the world's attention as a new source of global conflict and instability.

The history of the people of Nigeria as well as its politics is rooted in ethnic diversity. But Nigeria is not alone in this regard. Most countries today are multiethnic and multicultural. There are five main factors of ethnic diversity. These factors are race, tribe, ethnicity, religion and language. There are various degrees of combinations and intensity to which factors of diversity can manifest themselves and upon which their impact is felt in society. In much the same vein, each society tends to have different [sometimes similar] historical data to support the nature and source of its ethnic diversity. For example, the United States is noted for being ethnically diverse. Frequently cited sources of ethnic diversity in the United States relate to the 15th Century "African slave trade in Modern Europe and America" (Morse 1970, 8033) and the [ongoing] global political and religious persecution in Europe. Today, besides religious diversity, the United States is managing more diverse groups of people than any other country in the world. Predominantly, these ethnic groups include Whites, Blacks, Indians, Hispanics, Jews and Asians to name a few. In Nigeria ethnic diversity is based on prehistoric migration, its subsequent colonization and religion.

In the past, most people worldwide had viewed ethnic diversity as evil and adulterating. They tended to concentrate on people's differences rather than their similarities in spite of the humanistic and biologic consensus that all human beings are more alike than they are different. In recent years, however, overcoming the negative views of ethnic diversity, and building a "culture of borrowers and lenders" and of national purpose, allowing citizens of different persuasions to strive in harmony as a people is generally gaining the upper hand in most democratic societies.

Today, many nations are beginning to boast of more noble reasons why they are multicultural and multiethnic. In view of the global family concept, naturalization based on individual free choice to relocate and the refugee status based on regional, environmental and human disaster are some of the reasons given for human relocation having benefits for both the migrants and their host countries. Because of the inherent benefits in migration and ethnic diversity, well–to–do societies

USA: ETHNIC MIGRATION BY SELECTED CONTINENTS 1820–1972*

Excludes Native Americans

CONTINENTS	1951–1960	1961–1970	1969	1970	1971	1972
Europe	1,325,640	1,123,363	113,198	10,989	91,509	86,321
USSR	584	2,336	254	360	303	400
Asia	153,334	427,771	73,813	91,059	98,062	115,978
South America	996,944	1,716,374	164,045	161,727	171,680	173,165
Africa	14,092	28,954	4,460	7,099	5,844	5,472
Australia & New Zealand	11,506	19,562	2,278	2,693	2,357	2,550

Source: James A. Banks, <u>Teaching Strategies for Ethnic Studies</u>, 1975, Second Edition, Boston, Massachusetts, Allyn and Bacon, Inc., p.86–88

are generally viewed to manage as well as expand ethnic diversity better than poor societies.

Accordingly, countries such as the U.S., Germany, France, Canada and Great Britain to name a few, have been able to apply much of the economy of large population and other perspective of ethnic diversity to benefit their educational, social, economic and technological advancement. Yet it is an African proverb that has it that, " A man never walks backwards if he is going somewhere." Since the Industrial Revolution and the theory of the Invisible Hand by Adam Smith (1723–1790), most industrialized societies, having learned the concept of self–interest, political democracy, and the profit motive of the free enterprise systems have embraced socio–cultural diversity as the basis for collective and personal advancement in society. Most underdeveloped countries like Nigeria have not yet realized fully the importance of an integrative society for political, social and economic payoffs. For the most part, Nigeria is still a fragmented society by tribe, language and religion which in turn affects its economic future. Economically, Nigeria would benefit more from being an integrated rather than a divided group of producers and consumers of goods and services. Economics is the one aspect of life which does not generally discriminate between people in terms of their needs and wants that are obtained in the marketplace. The provision of human needs in the market place has the tendency of creating a stable and actualizing society.

In the United States for example, much of the social barriers for racial equality have been broken through legislations and economic activities that are available to meet human needs. Its constitution has stood tall as the supreme authority of the land from which an individual liberty and national unity are derived. Inherent in its constitution are numerous anti–discriminatory laws which to a large degree have both social and economic implications in that society. For example, the Fourteenth Amendment of its constitution guarantees that "No state shall deprive any person of life, liberty or property without the due process of the law: nor deny to any person within its jurisdiction the equal protection of the law." (Litka and Inman 1975, 121). The same amendment also prevents discrimination (anywhere) based on race, religion, creed, nationality or sexual orientation. Brown vs. Board of Education was likewise a landmark case that abolished school segregation in the U.S. giving every citizen equal opportunity to quality education as a cornerstone to fair competition in all aspects of civil life. The concept of the "melting pot" or, according to Jesse Jackson, the "rainbow" society is not only an achievable proposition, it is a concept of good common sense as many more societies are becoming multicultural and multiethnic. Its introduction into American social, educational and economic systems as a matter of moral principle was hoped to foster citizenship, individual aspiration, good neighborliness and national unity.

Consequently, each president such as the 7th American president, Andrew Jackson, and other policymakers over the years have made their mark in attempting to unify all Americans and maintain consistency in government through adherence to the Rule of Law and promotion of ethnic tolerance. The Jacksonian doctrine of individualism is not only consistent with the practice of capitalism and democracy but also famous for moving each American toward self-interest and self-determination within the umbrella of a larger society. In short, we view these efforts as the centerpiece for achieving a pluralistic democracy defined as a type of democracy whereby diverse interest groups of people have governed themselves through negotiation and compromise to fulfil human needs in society. Webster's Seventh New Collegiate Dictionary (1971,653) defines pluralism as a state of society in which members of diverse ethnic, racial, religious or social groups maintain an autonomous participation in and development of their traditional culture or special interest within the confines of a common civilization.

A few more words about a pluralistic democracy must be said. The difficulty of achieving a pluralistic democracy lies in the manner in which the pluralistic society itself is managed relative to moral leadership. Most social and political scientists would also agree that for a pluralistic society to function democratically and its government sustained, certain social prerequisites must be met. Some of these prerequisites, besides those already mentioned may include levels of literacy in society, freedom of publication and the press, and a viable irreproachable, irrevocable constitution.

The above prerequisites are also regarded as conditions likely to prevent indices of followership by blind faith. An educated society is an enlightened society about right and wrong and stability in society. Haines (1955) saw the connection between democracy and illiteracy particularly in Africa and wrote:

> It is generally agreed that democracy is a form of government which makes the biggest demands on the intelligence and watchfulness of its citizens. Some critics have therefore considered it hazardous that

self-government should be granted to Gold Coast and Nigeria when they have such a high degree of illiteracy" (p. 303).

John Stuart Mill –a British economist and philosopher (1806–1873)– was a leader of utilitarian movement who advocated an "individual liberty, the right of the minority and the need for public conscience" (*The New Lexicon Webster's Dictionary* 1989, 634). He also acknowledged an adverse impact of illiteracy on democracy. In much the same vein, Haines (1955) recommended that for democracy to succeed "universal education should precede universal enfranchisement" (p. 303). With regard to the fundamentals of democracy, Nigeria has tried to overcome most of its illiteracy problem through massive education campaigns dating back to 1963.

Even though the real take–off of "education expansion" in Nigeria is traced to the 1970's, education was recognized as the most important instrument of change soon after Nigeria's independence. Guidelines for the Fourth National Development Plan 1981–1985 has presented the following impressive statistics to support a rapid improvement in literacy rates in Nigeria. In the 1970's, education expansion affected all educational levels. Primary education enrollment in 1971 grew by an annual rate of ten percent to about 10.1 million pupils recorded for 1977–78 school year. Free–universal primary education programs were introduced intended for 11.5 million of enrollment in 1980. It however, reached its mark of 11.2 million in the 1977–78 school year. Secondary school enrollment grew from 489,000 in 1973–74 to 800,000 in 1977–78.

During the succeeding period, 800 additional secondary school facilities were built throughout the nation for anticipated additional enrollment of 1.5 million. Technical education which included polytechnics and colleges of technology had an enrollment figure of 3,000 in 1977 while in 1980 teacher education had enrollment figures of 234,680, students growing from 78,3777 in 1974–75 to 149,145 students in 1976–77. University education grew from 23,228 students in 1973–74 to 39,888 in 1976–77, and 47,000 in 1977–78. By 1988–89, a total enrollment in all universities by faculty, sex and levels of course was 172,404 students (*National Universities Commission – Nigeria, Annual Report* January 1989–December 1989 p.t–1.) Therefore, we hesitate to completely link the problem of Nigerian pluralistic democracy to illiteracy standards. The assumption is that in most parts of Nigeria, most Nigerians of 40 years of age in 1994 with

NIGERIA: ILLITERACY/LITERACY RATES 1962–1993

YEAR	AGE	TOTAL ILLITERACY	PERCENTAGE OF ILLITERACY	PERCENTAGE OF LITERACY
1962	15+	(100)	84.6	25.4
1976	15+	(100)	84.6	25.4
1977	15+	(100)	84.6	25.4
1984	15+	(100)	66.0	34.0
1985	15+	(100)	57.6	42.4
1993	15+	(100)	49.3	50.7

Source: Statistical Yearbook Illiteracy Population, UNESCO

average life expectancy at birth of 48 years (*World Population Data Sheet*, 1990) can read and write, and hence can participate effectively in a democratic process. Consequently, the lack of democracy and political stability in Nigeria can be linked to other causes.

In Nigeria, as well as in Africa as a whole, continuous work must be carried out to discern the impact of tribalism on the economic, political and social life of the masses. The result of such work should be in concert with utilitarian ideals which implies that ". . . the moral and political rightness of an action is determined by its utility defined as its contribution to the greatest good of the greatest number." (The New Lexicon Dictionary, p. 184). We feel that tribalism or ethnic hatred is not only counterproductive to development, but also inconsistent with utilitarianism.

Tribal or ethnic totalitarianism besides being oppressive has no civic and economic value in society. For example, between 1939–45, the problem of ethnic totalitarianism brought the world face to face with the worst hatred of one ethnic group toward another. Hitler's excessive favoritism of the "Aryan Aristocracy" –the so–called superior race– as well as his racial hatred toward the Jews is often regarded as the worst racial bigotry of all times worldwide (Gregor 1968, 179). So, when Hitler was defeated by the Allied Forces in 1945, Germany as well as the world was relieved of one source of ethnic intolerance. To this day, all Jewish people and lovers of freedom of association and domicile rights have not forgotten the irreparable racial injustice, and the holocaust always associated with the Nazi Germany.

It was no accident therefore, that in the same year, 1945, the United Nations (UN) decided against any forms of [ethnic] prejudice in society. Its charter was drafted to include respect for human rights and fundamental freedom, reiterating that every human being by mere birth has an equal right to education, life, liberty, and the pursuit of happiness. United Nation's effort was to forge a harmonious global family with the burden of protecting human beings from abuses. Under the UN Charter, independent nations were given the mandate to foster their citizens' fundamental liberties. But with the sovereign equality of nations and territorial integrity protection clauses, the UN has, many times, been reduced to a toothless bulldog, handicapped by its own laws. Accordingly, the problem of enforcing UN laws and regional laws and promptly bringing nations with human rights violations to justice has existed. Similar problems have been known to exist with regional organizations like Organization for African Unity (OAU), Organization of Arab States (OAS), etc.

With the end of the Cold war and the so-called super-power regional patrimony, the UN, as the only global patriot is perceived as starting to redefine its role, to play a more active role in promoting world peace and democracy. Its secondary role would include monitoring and collecting data on human rights abuses based on race, ethnicity, sex, religion, voting rights, and freedom of speech and of the press. In spite of its belated effort in Iraq, Bosnia, Somalia, China, South Africa, and so on in the late 1980s and early 1990s, the U.N. early intervention in the so-called "internal disputes" of member nations can be very crucial in preventing escalations of conflicts and Civil War. To be effective in this regards, the UN should have permanent offices in addition to human rights monitors in all member states in Africa to monitor tribal conflicts at their initial stages.

Unlike the U.S. or Germany, the socio-cultural conflict in Nigeria is not racial, but a mixture of tribal, religious and linguistic in component. In order to understand the intensity of socio-cultural diversity in any society such as Nigeria, the following questions are asked: What is a tribe or ethnicity? How does a tribe or ethnicity differ from a race? Of what relevance is tribalism, ethnic intolerance or racism to societal development? These questions need a complete investigation since their answers may provide an insight to Nigeria's, indeed Africa's, socio-political dilemma of the 20th Century.

Funk and Wagnall's Standard College Dictionary (1963) gave the following pertinent definitions of tribe, race and ethnicity respectively. "A tribe is a division, class or group of people especially a primitive or nomadic people usually characterized by a common ancestry, leadership, customs, etc. . . " (p. 1428). "A race is one of the major zoological subdivisions of mankind, regarded as having a common origin and exhibiting a relatively constant set of genetically determined physical traits. . . " (p. 1108). "Ethnicity is belonging to or distinctive of a particular racial, cultural or language division of mankind; also of or belonging to a population subdivision marked by common features of language, customs, etc. . ." (p. 455).

Wrightsman (1972) gave a technical definition of race and ethnic group respectively when he wrote:

> In essence, a race may be thought of as a population that is geographically contiguous and whose members breed together . . .

groups differing in culture, customs and language but not necessarily in physical characteristic —— are not called ethnic groups, they are considered different races. (p. 190)

Yet, there is another but rather crude method to define a race, tribe or ethnicity. The number of races in a given society are fewer than the number of tribes or ethnic groups. Ethnic groups are subdivisions of a race, so is a tribe; therefore, there exists some societies that are uni-racial but yet are multiethnic or multitribal. Nigeria is a Negroid, uni-racial but multi-tribal society. This assessment is true of many African societies. Other societies like the United States are predominantly multi-racial as was previously stated. Most anthropologists such as Ashley Montagu have classified humankind into four major races (human groups) as follows: "Negroid or Black, the Archaic white or Australoid, the Caucasoid or white and the Mongoloid" (Banks, 1979, 69–70).

Within the context of the above definitions, a tribe or an ethnic groups is discerned as a smaller subunit of human group having a more powerful force of human affinity than a race; usually being more catalystic, rigid and narrowly focused. This perhaps explains the basis for the intratribal cohesiveness believed to be the single destructive force to democracy in almost all African countries. In Nigeria, a lack of democracy for the most part, is seen within the context of inter-tribal division on one hand and intra-tribal cohesiveness on the other, i.e. most Nigerians ally more with their tribes than the nation. Rodney (1974, 227) stated that:

> One of the most important manifestations of historical arrest and stagnation of colonial Africa is that which commonly goes under the title of "tribalism." That term in its common journalistic setting is understood to mean that Africans have a basic loyalty to tribe rather than nation and that each tribe still retains a fundamental hostility towards its neighboring tribe. The examples favored by the capitalist press and bourgeois scholarship are those of Congo and Nigeria . . .

Yet, another writer stated that "on October 1, 1960, Nigeria became an independent monarchy within the commonwealth of nations...from the early days of independence, tribal antagonism and religious and political differences put serious strains on the unity of the federation" (Morse 1970, 6544). Tribalism is defined as those negative and divisive attitudes directed toward others based on tribal or ethnic origin. Over the years, Nigerian leaders have paid lip service to issues of tribalism. They have avoided to tackle it as a national emergency. The reason for the inactivity is that most of these leaders benefitted from tribalism. In an unpublished document, Dr. Okoh asserted that "in our society the question who gets what, when, and how, is generally predicated on ethnic criteria" (Okoh 1994, 3).

While we equate tribalism with racism as having "hate" as their common denominator; tribalism with narcissism, which according to Hall and Lindzey (1978) is described as "not really self love but self–inflation and over–evaluation owing to feelings of insecurities" (p. 176), we certainly can not describe the concept of tribe itself as new. The concept of tribes can be traced back to the Tribes of Israel of the pre–Christian era when "the tribal arrangement in Israel was based on descendants for the twelve sons of Jacob (Gen. 29:32–30:24;35:16–18). These 'twelve family heads. . .' produced the twelve tribes of Israel. . . Much of the organization of the Israelites revolve around the tribal structure" (*Aid to Bible Understanding* 1971,1614).

We feel therefore that it is possible for a person to be tribal without being tribalistic. A tribalistic person is one who practices tribalism (hate) while a tribal person is one who has awareness and pride in one's closet heritage. Marden and Meyer (1978) share Dr. James P. Comer's views on racism or tribalism by describing it as "a low level defense system and adjustment mechanism utilized by groups to deal with psychological and social insecurities" (p. 93) This feeling of insecurity is usually rooted in an irrational fear. There are two types of group fears in society. First, there is fear of losing a collective socio–economic status or opportunity in society. In our societies, social and economic status are inherent in the equality of education, jobs, housing and fair treatment under the law. There is also fear relating to sociopolitical domination such as the right to vote and the right to be voted for.

Encounters with any type of fear, unless intervened by stringent state laws is likely to foster the development of hate groups. Most social psychologists have argued that well–known hate groups like the Black Panther, the Ku Klux Klan (KKK), the Skinheads, the Hisbella, Hamas and the white supremacists of South Africa, all exhibit behaviors based on a defense mechanism acting as a protective jacket and promoting a false sense of superiority. This behavioral outcome can also be found among tribal hate groups as well.

Human beings could do well in our opinion if they learn to rid themselves of ethnic-, tribe-, and race–related insecurities. Contrary to Darwinism that believes in the survival of the fittest, and that one has to extort from his neighbor, throw the hardest punch and create as much confusion as possible in the name of survival, our experience tells us that Darwinistic attitudes when implemented prolongs hardship for mankind. Today, it has become a lot more difficult, even in a nuclear attack to annihilate an adversary group in order to usurp its belongings. Recent peace initiatives in the Middle East have painted a good picture that reaching out for a hand of friendship is better than fighting. So, Darwinism may be loosing its steam as a means of getting ahead in society. In our opinion, one can only meet the need for belongingness by providing belongingness possibilities for others. It is basically unequivocal that Nigeria, even today as well as in the past, has been on a constant political and economic roller coaster in spite of its abundant natural resources. As a result, nation–state formation seems to have completely eluded it to the extent that each political or military leader has come to rely on unitary factionalism and tribal fascism as a means of political and economic survival.

The problem of ethnic diversity is not unique to Nigeria alone. It is a worldwide issue needing a good effort on the part of national leaders and citizens alike, and international organizations to try to foster ethnic and racial coexistence based on the vision of two prominent American presidents --Thomas Jefferson and James Monroe whose belief in American unity can be emulated worldwide. Some of their advocacies for American solidarity and integration were contained in the following statements:

> To preserve the peace of our fellow citizens, promote their prosperity and happiness, reunite opinion, cultivate a spirit of candor, moderation, charity, and forbearance towards one another, are objects calling for the efforts and sacrifices of every good man and patriot. Our religion enjoins it; our happiness demands it; and no sacrifice is requisite but of passions hostile to both.
>
> It is a momentous truth, and happily of universal impression on the public mind, that our safety rests on the preservation of our Union.

> *Thomas Jefferson*
> *Letter of the General Assembly of Rhode Island*
> *and Providence Plantations, May 26, 1801.*

Our union is not held together by standing armies, or by any ties, other than the positive, interest and powerful attractions of its parts toward each other.

James Monroe, 5th President (1817 –25)
Message to Congress, May 4, 1822

Other early American political leaders worth emulating by Nigerian leaders with regards to national unity are George Washington, Andrew Jackson, John Quincy Adams, Franklin Pierce and William Henry Harrison. Their rudimental and patriotic steadfastness in American democracy and unity are still applicable to the American society to this day. We can only cite a few of their contributions for lack of space.

George Washington in his farewell address on September 19, 1796 stated:

It is of infinite moment that you should properly estimate the immense value of your national union to your collective and individual happiness; that you should cherish a cordial, habitual, and immovable attachment to it; accustoming yourselves to think and speak of it as of the palladium of your political safety and prosperity; watching for its preservation with jealous anxiety, discountenancing whatever may suggest even a suspicion that it can in any event be abandoned, and indignantly frowning upon the first dawning of every attempt to alienate any portion of our country from the rest or to enfeeble the sacred ties which now link together the various parts.

John Quincy Adams in his inaugural address on March 4, 1825 stated: The policy of our country is peace and the ark of our salvation. Still on the same subject of democracy and unity, William Henry Harrison in his inaugural address on March 4, 1841 stated:

It is union that we want, not a party for the sake of that party but a union of the whole country, for the defense of its interest and its honor against foreign oppression, for the defense of those principles for which our ancestors so gloriously contended.

THE "CONTINENT": COUNTRIES AND LOCATIONS

Chapter Four

Foreign Influence as a Subculture

Understanding the issues of foreign influence in Africa as a whole is the second logical step toward understanding its current socio-political and economic dilemma. These issues are contained in much of the literature dealing with the European and Arab early interest in Africa. Huntington (1968) introduced us to the concept of Radical Praetorianism as a means of understanding Africa's current problem. Specifically, he stated that:

> "a third source of radical Praetorianism is Western colonialism. In Africa . . . it weakened and often completely destroyed indigenous political institutions. Even when it took the form of "indirect rule," it undermined the traditional sources of legitimacy since the authority of the native rulers were clearly dependent on the power of the imperialist state" (pp. 199–200).

Because Africa had their well–developed traditions and lifestyles prior to the arrival of foreign intruders, imported folkways, religion and language subcultures only served to produce what Professor Ali Mazrui now calls "African Triple Heritage." The bastardization of Africa by foreign intruders of the 15th and 16th centuries has no doubt resulted in identity crises among most Africans and African leaders. Redefining oneself amidst the combined influence of Europe, Arabia and Africa has been an uphill battle. This has affected Africa's political leadership the most. There is also a psycho–social enslavement of the human mind which goes along with the whole notion that Europe or Arabia is better than Africa – to live, go to school, bank money and escape to when one is in trouble at home. This defeatist attitude by African elites does not lend itself to the hope of Africa's liberation.

Nyerere (1974) advocated African liberation from past political and economic totalitarianism of the colonialists. He then went on to distinguish the colonial totalitarian leadership from the type of political leadership and guidance that Africa needed to liberate itself. According to Nyerere, this new African leadership would be based on "talking, discussing with people, explaining and persuading...that everyone must be allowed to speak freely and everyone must be listened to" (Nyerere 1974, 29–30). In spite of Nyerere's guidelines and initiatives to leadership in Africa, Africa has become a breeding ground of African despots who are socially, politically and psychologically dressed in colonial robes in the treatment of their people as well as their concern for democracy. In an article entitled: Nigeria Suffers in Silence, Buckley (1995, A1) pointed out that:

> Gen. Sani Abacha's war against opponents of his military government...has crushed labor unions and shut down nearly 20 newspapers and magazines. His security forces have arrested dozens of activists, killed scores of Nigerians in demonstrations...

SCRAMBLE FOR AFRICA

"Historically, much of Africa has been the scene of a long series of migrations and invasions of foreigners from the Phoenicians, Greeks, Romans, Arabs, Indians, Italians, and Turks to the Western Europeans" (Harris 1972, 185). As early as the 15th century, many European expeditions were carried out around the West Coast of Africa. The well known expeditions were those led by Prince Henry the Navigator of Portugal in 1434 and Vasco da Gama which ended in 1498. Besides the taking of slaves of African ancestry, European settlements were established in various parts of Africa, encouraged by "the knowledge of the wealth to be obtained in the region (Morse 1970, 217). But, between 146 BC and 114 AD, the mediterranean Africa including Egypt was part of the Roman Empire.

The history of ancient Egypt is in some great measure a gateway to understanding the rest of African history. For example, the conquest of Egypt in North Africa by the Arab in 642 AD was geographically significant as the first step of Muslim influence in Africa as a whole. Harris (1972,47) reported that: "Islam's expansion into Egypt in 639, the muslim destruction of Adulis in 710, and the establishment of Umayyad control over Dahlak Island in 715 signaled a new era for northeastern Africa. . . ."

Thereafter in 1517, the powerful mohammadans – the Turks after overrunning Egypt "made Algeria, Tunisia and Tripoli provinces of the Turkish Empire" (p. 217) before pushing southwards. In addition to establishing trade depots in different parts of the continent, the mohammedans also built mosques where Koranic education was propagated. Seldom have writers described the Arabs as colonizers in their reporting the history of foreigners in Africa. The Arab influence within the general scheme of things was as seductive as the influence of their European counterparts. The reason for not classifying the Arabs as colonialists is explainable. Unlike Christianity which sought to transplant Europe to Africa by force, Islam's approach to occupy Africa was rather subtle. Islam's recognition of and identification with certain core African cultures such as marriage customs (polygamy), and its initial help in resisting westernized education and values not only created a sense of brotherhood among most Africans but also helped to exonerate them from the stigma of colonialism.

Italian expansion in Africa did not begin until after WWI (1914–1918). Through separate negotiations, Italy gained ownership of Libya, Italian Somaliland and the kingdom of Ethiopia. From the 16th up to the early 20th centuries, territorial acquisition in Africa by foreigners had become routine and rather feverish. In short, Africa was exposed to fierce competition between the Arabs and the Europeans, initially for trade purposes. It was the UN's charter after WWII in 1945 promoting "respect for human rights and fundamental freedom" that slowed down the madness of the scramble for occupation of Africa and paved the way for African political self determination. The Portuguese and the British interest in Nigeria were greater than those of the other European rivalries. Arabian commercial activity which was not very ambitious was limited to Northern Nigeria. They traded in such commodities as frankincense, myrrh, coffee, dates, and pearls. Meanwhile, other trading routes were developed most especially by Britain when "palm oil became so important as an article of commerce that the delta region became known as the oil rivers: British counsel was sent to Lagos and in 1861 Great Britain took full possession of that area" (Morse 1970,

6544) and adopted "a system of indirect rule through the native chiefs" (The Encyclopedia America: The International Reference Work 1958, 220–222).

PARTITION AND COLONIZATION OF AFRICA

In 1875, at the Berlin Conference in Germany, Africa was unilaterally partitioned among Great Britain, France, Portugal, Netherlands, Spain, Germany, Belgium and Italy under the leadership of King Leopold II of Belgium who was considered as a "Christian colonizer" (Clarke 1991, 19). This lack of consultation with the Africans to partition Africa was an ongoing mindlessness of the colonialists about Africa as a whole. Ironically, Africa was regarded as primitive by European standards, therefore, needing proselytizing. Consequently, the meeting of 1876 was to determine the best method to achieve this objective. It was therefore necessary that Christian missionaries be brought in to systematically implement the 3–M method of European occupation of Africa namely merchant, missionaries and lastly mercenaries to protect their loot. It was important that the 3–M system be adopted. But in order for the 3–M system to succeed, the approach had to be both surreptitious and imperceptible. It was also important that a proper order in which the 3–M system would apply be adequately followed. Most people who know how Africa was colonized would agree that chronologically speaking, it was the merchants who arrived first, then the missionaries and lastly the mercenaries. Of the three groups, the missionaries can be regarded as the disciple of change.

Much has already been said about the Europeans' commercial interest in Africa. Let us examine in some detail why European missionaries and mercenaries were important during and after the colonialists' occupation of Africa. One must remember that the Europeans arrived in Africa with an aloof master–servant attitude. Everything African was beneath the dignity of its oppressor. In this case, it was necessary for the colonialists to be self–sufficient upon arrival in Africa and to be prepared to teach the servant the likes and dislikes of the master. Acculturation was one sure way to African

EUROPEAN SELF SUFFICIENCY AND THE MEANING OF 3–M IN AFRICA

MERCHANTS	Agriculture
	Buying (domestic)
	Selling (domestic)
	Imports (Export investment)

↑↓

MISSIONARIES	Lifestyle changes
	Indoctrination
	Acculturation
	Education (4R's)
	Religion and Behaviorism

↑↓

MERCENARIES	Militia for domestic emergency (Her Majesty police force
	Militia for foreign emergency (Her Majesty military force)
	Acculturation
	Indoctrination
	Expansionism
	Superior [vs. inferiority complexes]

subjugation. The colonialists had to raise indigenous militia, police and military for domestic and foreign emergencies. Many colonial subjects participated in world wars especially WWII. Until 1960 Nigerians, for example, were regarded on paper as British subjects with the eligibility to fight and defend British interest globally. The colonialists had two basic plans to execute in Africa. The first plan was the initial motive and the outline of activities. The second plan was the methodology of control.

As contained in *Encyclopedia America: The International Reference Work* (1958,222), the European overall activity in Africa is summarized as:

1. Early maritime exploration
2. Penetration of the interior
3. Formation of trading company
4. Arrival of the missionaries
5. Assumption of government control
6. Rivalry and warfare between governments followed by partition of Africa into political areas
7. A period of exploitation of natives and their natural resources
8. A time of better political adjustment between Africa and European with Africans achieving some measure of self–government

In order for Europe to transplant its ideologies fully to Africa, the 3–M System of Control and pacification, namely merchants, missionaries and mercenaries was employed. Eurocentric education had become the biggest weapon to use; utilizing the so–called 4–R system of education –rithmetic, riting, reading and religion. Of the 4–r's, religion was the most potent weapon of pacification and control – the one area which the colonialists had to burn the most midnight oil. African deity and methods of worship were soon replaced by the Bible and the notion of saving the soul. In other words, going to heaven after death was to become a more important human life achievement than national wealth, more important than the technological know–how or social skills needed to acquire them. It is important for African posterity to know why social and technical skills were not stressed in the colonial educational curriculum despite the Industrial Revolution of the 18th and 19th centuries which swept Europe demanding "mechanization of industry and the subsequent changes in social and economic organization, especially in Britain" (*The New Lexicon Webster Dictionary*, 1989,495).

Initially, Africans were not to be educated beyond the present day grade or secondary school levels. After all, Africans were only to perform clerical, semi–skilled or unskilled labor. For a long while, Africans were messengers, gardeners, doorkeepers, cooks, nannies, mail carriers, valets, etc. The goal of colonial education was not to liberate Africa economically or prepare it for self government but to enhance Europe's continued occupation and economic interests. Haines (1955,298) pointed that,

> the lack of personnel and technical knowledge is in part a legacy of the lack of a clearly defined policy of education under the British adminnce as a Subcultureof this, the educational system was not sufficiently geared to the social needs and goals of the people.

It is therefore not surprising that most writers who have opinions on colonization of African people have continued to link the post–colonial decay of Africa to the intentional underdevelopment that took place under European occupation of Africa. For example, Garvey (1986,66) stated that "the native Africans unfortunately have not been schooled in the appreciation of the valuable mineral wealth in Africa." He went on to say that while the "white man" used his high technology to exploit African mineral wealth such as diamonds for his own benefit, Africans were limited to rubber tapping. Africans were also prevented from cultivating the soil – all of which resulted in Africa's underdevelopment. There are opinions that Africans' early non–involvement in determining their economic and political destiny has contributed to their current lackadaisicalness in such matters as total self liberation.

There are other consequences of colonial activities in Africa. The early taking from Africa and nothing put back into its economy created Africa's dependency on Europe and its subsequent position of economic and social disadvantage. The late Jomo Kenyatta of Kenya then responded broadly to this problem when he once said to his people that 'when the white man came, we had the land, and they had the book. The taught us to pray with our eyes closed. When we opened them, we had the book – and they had the land' (Halford 1994,8).

Throughout the period of occupation, Africans had continued to be suspicious of the colonialists motives. Though helpless, Africans were not naive. They understood the injustices of the colonial rule. But they were helpless because their level of self determination was controlled by the invaders' psycho–religious and commercial forces. It is worthy of note that slave trading between Africa and America was oftentimes approved by church high officials after bringing Africans under Christian influence. David Livingstone, for example, was a Scottish missionary and an African explorer (1813–73) who openly condemned European double dealing between religion and illicit commercial interest. In Africa, mission schools were built to perpetuate European values no matter how much they conflicted with African traditional values. In Nigeria, for example, the first English speaking mission school was founded at Badagry near Lagos in about 1842. The nearness of this mission school to a river outlet (still in existence) is indicative of the interrelationship between education, religion, and illicit trade during the colonial era.

To achieve full conformity with Europe, Nigerians had to abandon, or at least minimize their native tongue to accommodate a foreign language as a medium of classroom instruction and also in church worship. Eurocentric education and religion in Nigeria and in other parts of Africa were inseparable, but in countries like the United States where education was progressive, the practice had been the "separation of church and state" i.e., education and religion did not mix. In Africa, it was almost mandatory for those who attended mission schools to be devout Christians inspite of religious liberalism that was taking place in Europe at that time. In the case of Catholicism one had to attend Mass every morning and also remember to "keep the Sabbath holy" by attending Sunday mass. Catholic mass was conducted usually in the dialect of Rome. Latin was taught in schools and was to be mastered by the natives. Other church denominations had different protocols and methods of training Africans to be religious, reverent and receptive. According to the Bible, Baptism was necessary to remove the original sin from an individual. At baptism it was both the water and a foreign name, not water and an African name that exonerated the child from his original sin. This wave of education and the demand to adapt to it still has both a lasting and confounding effect on Africa's traditional religions. It also affected much of the Afrocentric consciousness and dependency propensity in general to the extent that "the native educated in the mission school was unfit to live in European or the native society" (Haines 1955, 168). According to most social scientists, there is a correlation between education, standard of living, and productivity.

COMPARISON OF DEVELOPMENT INDICATORS BETWEEN FORMER EUROPEAN COLONIZERS AND THEIR FORMER AFRICAN COLONIES OVER 5 MILLION IN POPULATION

COUNTRIES *former colonies () former colonizers	PER CAPITA INCOME IN US$	POPULATION ESTIMATE IN MILLIONS	BIRTH RATE/ 1000	DEATH RATE/ 1000	LIFE EXPT. AT BIRTH IN YEARS	% POP. UNDER AGE 15	INFANT MORTALITY/1000 LIVE BIRTHS	% POP. OVER 65	INDEPEND- ANCE YEAR
*ALGERIA (FRANCE)	2,450 16,080	25.6 56.4	40 14	9 9	60 77	46 20	74 7.5	4 14	1962
*MOROCCO (SPAIN)	750 7,740	25.6 39.4	35 11	10 8	50 77	42 22	82 9.0	4 13	1956
*COTE DIVOIRE (FRANCE)	740 16,080	12.6 56.4	51 14	14 9	53 77	49 20	96 7.5	2 14	1960
*GHANA (BRITAIN)	400 12,800	15.0 57.4	44 14	13 12	55 75	45 19	86 9.5	3 15	1957
*NIGERIA (BRITAIN)	290 12,800	118.8 57.4	46 14	17 12	48 75	45 19	121 9.5	2 15	1960
*SENEGAL (FRANCE)	630 16,080	7.4 56.4	46 14	19 9	46 77	44 20	128 7.5	3 14	1960
*KENYA (BRITAIN)	360 12,800	24.6 57.4	46 14	7 12	63 75	50 19	62 9.5	2 15	1963
*MOZAMBIQUE (PORTUGAL)	100 3,670	15.2 10.4	45 12	19 10	47 74	44 22	141 14.9	3 13	----.
*TANZANIA (GERMANY)	160 18,503	26.0 63.2	51 11	14 11	49 76	49 15	106 7.5	2 15	1961

COUNTRIES *former colonies ( )former colonizers	PER CAPITA INCOME IN US$	POPULATION ESTIMATE IN MILLIONS	BIRTH RATE/ 1000	DEATH RATE/ 1000	LIFE EXPT. AT BIRTH IN YEARS	% POP. UNDER AGE 1	INFANT MORTALITY/1000 LIVE BIRTHS	% POP. OVER 65	INDEPEND-ANCE YEAR
*CAMEROON (FRANCE)	1,010 16,080	11.1 56.4	42 11	19 9	46 77	44 20	125 7.5	3 12	1960
*ZAIRE (FRANCE)	170 16,080	36.6 56.4	47 14	14 9	53 77	46 20	125 7.5	3 14	1960
*UGANDA (BRITAIN)	280 12,800	18.0 57.4	52 14	17 12	49 75	49 19	107 9.5	2 15	1962
**SOUTH AFRICA (NETHERLANDS)	2,290 14,530	39.6 14.9	35 13	8 8	63 77	40 18	55 7.6	4 13	---
*CHAD (FRANCE)	160 16,080	5.0 56.4	44 14	20 9	46 77	43 20	132 7.5	4 14	1960
*ZIMBABWE (GERMANY)	660 18,530	9.7 63.2	42 11	10 11	58 77	45 15	72 7.5	3 15	---
*MALAWI (BRITAIN)	160 12,800	9.2 57.4	52 14	18 12	49 75	48 19	130 9.5	3 15	1964
*EGYPT (BRITAIN)	650 12,800	54.7 57.4	38 14	9 12	60 75	41 19	90 9.5	4 15	1922
*NIGER (FRANCE)	310 16,080	7.9 56.4	51 14	21 9	45 77	47 20	135 7.5	3 14	1960
*MALI (FRANCE)	230 16,080	8.1 56.4	52 14	22 9	45 77	47 20	117 7.5	3 14	1960
*GUINEA (FRANCE)	350 16,080	7.3 56.4	47 14	22 9	42 77	43 20	147 7.5	3 14	1958

COUNTRIES *former colonies ()former colonizers	PER CAPITA INCOME IN US$	POPULATION ESTIMATE IN MILLIONS	BIRTH RATE/ 1000	DEATH RATE/ 1000	LIFE EXPT. AT BIRTH IN YEARS	% POP. UNDER AGE 15	INFANT MORTALITY/1000 OF LIVE BIRTHS	% POP. OVER 65	INDEPEND- ANCE YEAR
*BURKINA FASO (FRANCE)	230 16,000	9.1 56.4	50 14	18 9	51 77	48 20	126 7.5	4 14	1960
*TUNISIA (FRANCE)	1,230 16,080	8.1 56.4	28 14	7 9	65 77	39 20	59 7.5	4 14	--- 14
*BARUNDI (BELGIUM)	230 14,550	5.6 9.9	48 12	15 11	51 74	45 18	114 9.2	3 14	1962
*SUDAN (BRITAIN)	340 12,800	25.2 57.4	45 14	16 12	50 75	45 19	108 9.5	3 15	1956
*MADAGASCA (FRANCE)	180 16,080	12.0 56.4	46 12	14 9	54 77	45 20	120 7.5	3 14	---
*RWANDA (BELGIUM)	310 14,550	7.3 9.9	51 12	17 11	49 75	49 18	122 9.2	2 14	---
*SOMALIA (ITALY/BRITAIN)	170 13,320	8.4 57.7	51 10	20 9	45 75	47 18	132 9.5	3 14	1960
*ZAMBIA (BRITAIN)	290 12,800	8.1 57.4	51 14	14 12	53 75	49 19	80 9.5	2 15	1964
*ANGOLA (PORTUGAL)	---- 3,670	8.5 10.4	47 12	20 10	45 74	45 22	137 14.9	3 13	---

*FORMER COLONIES   () FORMER COLONIZERS

Source: 1990 Population Data Sheet, Population Reference Bureau Inc., Washington, D.C.

People with low standard of living are subject to be dependent on others for their livelihood. This concern has been cited in many of Human Capital literature such as *The Wealth of Nations* by Adam Smith which advocated economic prosperity through self-interest, etc. In much the same vein, Julius Nycrere of Tanzania had concern about faulty education in Africa and launched "education for self-reliance" in 1967 in lieu of "book learning" which characterized colonial education.

In addition to faulty colonial education, Nigeria also suffered an economic exploitation under colonization, notably from Lugard's (1914–1919) policy of the Dual Mandate in which African resources was to be used to develop the world. According to an African proverb, when a tree is hewn down, it usually lies where it fell. Unfortunately this African proverb did not come to fulfillment under the colonial occupation. To carry out the initial economic castration and faulty education, the colonialists under Lugard's administration in Nigeria embarked on:

> A trade economy. From the time that Britain began her conquest and occupation of Nigeria, she had regarded its colonies in Africa as underdeveloped estates whose resources would be tapped for the development of her own economy. This concept of the role of the economy of the African colonies was redefined and given a moral justification by Lugard in his dual mandate when he said that the colonial economy was to be exploited by the benefit of mankind (National Youth Service Corps 1973, 81).

The first system of colonial administration in Nigeria was the Indirect [Rule] Administration sometimes referred to as a policy of "divide and rule." According to this system native authorities were appointed to native courts and other administrative agencies to protect British judiciary, administrative and economic interests, and to supplement for European personnel shortages experienced in the three occupied protectorates of Niger Delta, Colony and Protectorate of Lagos, and the Northern Protectorates.

Thomas Hodgkins (1957) reported that in addition to keeping African traditional authorities under the thumb of the British administrator, Indirect Rule policies were famous in producing just a handful of arrogant educated African elites who usually rejected the traditional authorities as "unenlightened, incompetent and British-inspired." These traditional rulers were themselves "largely excluded form the exercise of genuine leadership" (pp. 46–47) during the colonial rule. The fact that Africans have continued to receive Eurocentric education even after independence is reflected not only in the civilian but in the unpatriotic attitudes of the African military leaders. For example, most officers in the Nigerian military are often quoted as receiving their military training abroad. These leaders tend to lack the idealistic prerequisites and the necessary inclinations to develop their nations. Instead, they tend to follow elitist and social inequality policies similar to that of the colonizers.

It must be remembered that British conquest, occupation and development of Nigeria took place in stages. Each protectorate followed separate goals and policies, creating a developmental disparity between each segment of the Nigerian society. The effect of following different goals and policies impacted differently in Nigeria's North and South. Educationally, Northern traditional rulers unlike their Southern counterparts did not trust Westernized education and were not immediately receptive to it. Northern mistrust of the "European Infidel" was based on religious grounds. This reason had somehow forced colonial authorities in the short term to exercise restraint in dismantling Northern traditional values and the existing Koranic School system which had at the time a sizable enrollment.

In 1899, Frederick Lugard who was often regarded as tough and ruthless was sent to the Northern protectorate to solve the rejection problem which Britain had suffered in the North. As far back as January 1, 1900, he had made Lokoja his headquarters in a bouncing ceremony, hoisted the British flag there and declared to the Caliph and all the Emirs that he was the ruler of the Caliphate. The implication of Lokoja episode was the changing of the natural boundary between North and South -- a calculated attempt to curry favor from the Muslims who had flatly rejected to be ruled by infidels. Consequently modern and Westernized education as we know it today undoubtedly took a slower pace in the bigger North than in the smaller South.

In essence, Arab and European modernization in Nigeria as a whole had created two separate and unequal societies. Umoren (1989, 18) stated that:

> Mission education stopped where Islam prevailed in Northern Nigeria. The historical differential access to modern education between Northern and Southern Nigeria may be traced to the colonial policy which discouraged any attempt by the missionaries to dismantle the existing educational system in the North.

In the *1968 Nigerian School Directory*, it is also stated that:

> Islam had made several converts in certain part of Nigeria before Christian missions arrived. But the Islamic schools gave religious instruction. By 1913, there were 19,073 of these Koranic schools with about 143,312 pupils in Northern Nigeria (1968, 1).

By the late 1950s, North was already behind in most areas of human endeavor where Christian education was a prerequisite. Coleman (1958) maintained that by 1957 the combined Christian primary/secondary school enrollment in the South was 2,371,525 with a total of 13,649 schools while the North had 189,127 school enrollment in 2,098 schools (see Coleman p.134). Educational and economic disparities in Nigeria, can be argued from two divergent points. First, Northern protectorate made a conscious choice to follow Arabic school curriculum which was perceived to be less progressive than Eurocentric school curriculum in preparing men and women for the world of work. Hodgkin (1957,94) shed more light on this problem when he wrote:

> Equally, the extent to which Islam has tended to assist, or check, the rise of nationalism in various regions in which it is a force, demands closer study. The links which Islam provides, particularly through hajj, with Asian peoples and ideas: its capacity to transcend colonial frontiers; its freedom from racialism, and from political association with imperial Europe – such factors enable Islam to appeal in a special way to Africans in this period of national awakening. On the other hand the effectiveness of Islam as a stimulus is limited by the conservatism of its orthodox spiritual leaders, and by the formalism of traditional Koranic education.

Second, the educational disparity that went far beyond 1914 seemed a deliberate act by the colonial masters to plant a seed of discourse between the North and the South, realizing that education is the liberator and equalizer of people. Kneller (1971,378) stated that: "Education is a critical component in determining life chances as well as in preparing persons to cope with the demands of the larger society."

By 1960, 46 years later, the amalgamated Nigeria was still buried in the same economic, social and political malaise, and in 1994 almost 80 years after the Amalgamation date, North and South cannot still live in harmony. The historical events that created these circumstances can not be ignored as Nigeria looks ahead. But thus far any policy towards educational parity in Nigeria has been a painful exercise especially when it usually involved set–aside and hold–back programs in public funding of education. The main argument usually lay in a formula that would not punish or reward a people whose mode of behavior is over 100 years old and ought to have been changed where necessary. National Youth Service Corps (1973,78) however acknowledged that:

> although the differential in educational development as between the North and South constitutes a major problem of national building today, it is only when we understand the historical setting which has created this differential that we can meaningfully seek to offset the differential without bitterness, without arrogance and without rancour.

African modernization and the unequal development under colonial occupation had yet another implication in addition to the economic and social inequality in Nigeria as well as in other parts of Africa. According to Huntington (1969) African tribalism started with colonization. Before the arrival of the European to modernize Africa, indigenous Africans enjoyed communal life which had become the basis of African socialist movement of the early 1960's. Huntington (1968, 38) stated that: "So also in much of African tribal consciousness was almost unknown in traditional rural life. Tribalism was a product of modernization and the impact on a traditional society."

By moving away from the traditional social life, African people began to formulate themselves into pockets of ideological groups of strong tribal identities. Consequently, the concept of tribal preservation developed and became pervasive. It can be said that group (tribe) consciousness can work both positively and negatively in society. Accordingly, if the development of group consciousness can lead to political institutions, larger organization and into national unity, that would be positive. On the contrary, if group consciousness is delimited to tribal or ethnic levels of society, it could make attaining national unity rather difficult.

Specifically since Independence, Nigeria has experienced ethnic disunity which is caused by its policy of defacto Indirect Rule – a system which tends to strengthen tribal chiefs, raise their comfort levels and status to the extent that they become disinterested to conceptualize national unity. This observation had perhaps led Huntington (1969) to conclude that:

Group consciousness however can also be a major obstacle to the creation of effective political institutions encompassing a broader spectrum of social forces . . . and along with group prejudices comes group conflict. Ethnic or religious groups which had lived peacefully side by side in traditional society became aroused to violent conflict as a result of the interaction, the tensions, the inequalities generated by social and economic modernization (p. 39).

Parmele (1994, A23) also maintained that:

Much of Africa's tribal conflict can be blamed on the inheritance of highly centralized states that in standard colonial divide and rule style, delegated most power to a favored tribe or tribes. After Independence, this characteristic evolved into political systems in which the winner usually the dominant ethnic group —took all and losers got precious little.

RELIGION AND LANGUAGE SUBCULTURE

Idiomatically speaking, Islam and Christianity even in modern Africa can sometimes be likened to two half brothers with tremendous ideological differences between them. The Biblical story of Isaac and Ishmael [the seed of Abraham] serves as an important frame of reference to apply to Nigerian religious, social and political life. To put the above analysis in perspective Haines (1955, 91) stated: "It is not practicable to bracket Islam and Christianity together . . . because they differ greatly in nature, influence and geographical distribution." In Nigeria, Islam is believed to be predominantly practiced in the North and sparsely in the West while Christianity is practiced predominantly in the East and sparsely in the West. In Lagos and in other metropolitan cities there tend to be a mixture of both Muslims and Christians.

Generally speaking, the official language of Islam (Koran) as an organized religion is Arabic while the official language of Christianity (Bible) is Hebrew translated into English language and quite lately into other native dialects. It is noteworthy that these religious groups tend to have the language of their religion as their official language of business and classroom instruction also. This means that people's lifestyles, values, group norms, beliefs are closely associated with and draw meaning from the religion they practice.

As far as Nigerian religious groups are concerned, except for those who practice indigenous religion, Mecca is for the Muslims as Jerusalem is for the Christians as the ultimate holy place of worship and paying of homage to their religious ancestors. Over the years, many Nigerians have lost sight of the fact that Islam is as foreign to Nigeria as Christianity. Nigerians have allowed themselves to be sidetracked from the important realities of nation building. This loss of focus has been linked for the most part to much of the age–long disagreements between two religious factions in Nigeria – the christian south and muslim north. Chancellor Williams in *The Destruction of Black Civilization* has shed more light on the influence of foreign religion on African race. His explanation on this subject should not go without notice for fear of missing an important historical information of great significance to Nigeria's social and political instability. Williams (1987, 22–3) stated that:

> the relentless searchlight of history were turned on the roles played by both Islam and Christianity in the subjugation of the Blacks. This confused many and outraged those who did not pause to distinguish evil men who use religion to disguise their real aims. The unthinking Muslim and Christian would believe that his religion is being attacked rather than those conquerors and enslavers who disgraced it in covering their drive for wealth and world domination.

In Northern Nigeria, Arabic influence gained grounds through trade, Koranic language, Koranic religion, Koranic education and intermarriages, while European influence through similar mechanisms was increasing its spheres and taking root in the South. Mazrui (1986, 89) stated that "in Northern Nigeria, linguistic influence. . . have found their way into the Hausa language which is spoken not only by Hausa but by those Fulani who have settled in Hausa towns and villages." Even though most Northerners speak Arabic today, some have managed to retain their native dialect; the same goes with the Southerners with regards to English. But to most Islamic faithfuls, population size tends to be more important than their linguistic affiliation. Self identity is also an important step to group identity unto the territorial identification and acquisition. The same principle can be said about Christianity.

So, when one critically looks at Nigeria, one is likely to see two colossal forces each struggling either for domination or survival. These two forces are like two elephants fighting in the jungle. From an African standpoint, whenever two heavy weights collide, it is the grass under their feet that is always left in ruin. This tends to be one of Nigeria's dilemma --the ideological differences between religious and cultural groups which are adversely affecting the larger group cohesiveness. A few incidences of religious hatred and bigotry in Nigeria have been cited by many writers including T.C. McCaskie (1994) in *Recent History of Nigeria* as contained in Africa South of the Sahara. In 1987 there was fierce fighting between Muslim and Christian youths at Kafanchan in which there were many injured and deaths. In 1990 a military mutiny and the seizure of the Federal Radio Corporation headquarters by a junior army officer, Maj. Gideon Orkar, was followed by his suggestion that Muslim states of Sokoto, Borno, Katsina, Kano and Bauchi be 'excised' from Nigeria. In 1991, there were a number of demonstrations based on some publication which was regarded as blasphemous by the muslim group. As a result, many Christians were killed at Bauchi.

In 1991, another demonstration in Kano by the muslims protesting a tour of the state by a christian preacher turned violent. In this clash between Christian and Muslim, many people were reported killed before the military could intervene. In January 1992 there was violence when Muslim fundamentalists demonstrated and demanded in Katsina an imposition of islamic law (*Shariá*). In February of the same year, there was yet another clash in Kaduna between Hausa ethnic Muslims and *Kataf* – the Christians. The implication of imported religion on African aspiration had already been discussed. Based on the aforesaid, Nigeria is only another victim of a borrowed lifestyle. But neither "Jesus Christ (between 8 and 4 – about 29 AD) – the central figure of Christianity, born in Bethlehem in Judea" (Morse 1970, 5224) nor Muhammad (AD 570?–632) "the founder of the islamic religion. . .born in Mecca in southwestern Arabia" (The World Book Encyclopedia 1986, 7546) had proposed that (Africans) Nigerians destroy themselves in the name of religion, despite the genealogical animosity of Isaac and Ishmael – the seeds of Abraham. Incidentally, both Christ and Muhammad taught morality and compassion as implied in the *Sermon on the Mount* and *The Six Articles of Faith* respectively.

Accordingly, the numerous religions conflicts which can be linked to Nigeria's social, political and economic decay do not reflect the teaching of Christ or Muhammad. Rather, they reflect the personal ambition of those Nigerians who are bent on using religion as a springboard for power, influence and politico–tribal domination. As a matter of repetition and for the social wellbeing of Nigeria, religion of

any kind must be kept out of politics. Religion neverth.
unique place in the Nigerian society. But, because Nigeria ⅃
theocratic state, co–mingling of religion in state matters is likely
create social tension. Each and every Nigerian should have the freedom
to practice his faith wisely without interfering with the civil liberty of
others. Freedom of religion should mean that every Nigerian can
legitimately practice the religion of his choice without interference,
within the law in any part of Nigeria.

AMALGAMATION OF NORTHERN
AND SOUTHERN NIGERIA

In 1906, southern Nigeria, which was comprised of east, midwest,
Lagos and its surrounding states became the colony and the protectorate
of Southern Nigeria. Becasue of its large size and shortage of European
staff, this area was placed under the ruling of native authorities.
Thereafter, in 1914, Lugard pursued a centralized form of administration
by amalgamating southern and northern territories, hitherto distinct and
separate, into one Nigeria.

Some scholars have cited the issue of amalgamation as an attempt
to bridge the economic and educational disparities of the South and
North while others who view all colonial activities in Africa as gold–
digging have continued to cite an imperial administrative convenience
as the sole motive for Lugard's action. One source has however,
summarized Lugard's intent of the amalgamation as "the need to find an
answer to the economic problems of the protectorates of the Northern
Nigeria than by any particular wish to bring the people of Nigeria into
a single meaningful unit" (National Youth Service Corps 1973, 78). The
mere fact that these Nigerian entities were encouraged to follow
separate and unequal developments underscores Lugard's motive and
ambition in Nigeria and helps in understanding what kind of a person
he was. Was Lugard a good or an evil man? Some writers have called
him a bully. Clarke (1991, 72) in his description of Lugard stated:

> Let me tell you what Cecil John Rhodes, Dr. Lander Starr Jameson
> and others did to my people in South Africa (Monomotapa) when
> they brought in Captain John Lugard, who made Hitler look like a
> sissy boy. Lugard was exterminating the Indians in India by the
> million. They brought him to do the same in South Africa, and
> moved him from there to what was later called Nigeria Protectorate.

ıstration in Nigeria, native Nigerians did not
ılized government until after the 1922
ıded for a total of 46 of both official and
ıs. Even though this constitution was to allow
ıte in government, many decisions regarding
of the protectorates were made in London by
ıe implication here is that even though self–
ıted to some African countries including Nigeria,
such a ᵍ⸱   "far from involving any total surrender of British
power in West Aı..ca" (Hodgkin 1957,42). As such, Nigerian natives
were not adequately trained to benefit from such participation since
Britain did not contemplate future independence for Nigeria at that time.
If Nigerians were allowed full participation with responsibility in
administering their own social and political affairs, they might have
learned, informally, pertinent skills that would later prove useful to
them. Such an accommodation of the natives to learn the truth about
democracy and the working of capitalism would undermine the ambition
of the colonialists' policy of territorial occupation. It was important that
a system of representation without responsibility be used instead. But
such lack of effective and full participation had become a source of
motivation to Nigerians which resulted in cultural nationalism as
implied in Richard's and Macpherson's constitutions of 1947 and 1951
respectively. In both of these constitutions, Britain was compelled to
adopt a step by step transfer of power to the natives based on the
tripartite regions. Nigeria's decolonization was also caused by the
impact of WWII and the UN Charter on Basic Human Rights and
Freedom.

In 1939, Southern Nigeria was split into Eastern and Western
provinces (later regions) by the succeeding governor –– Bourdillon
while the Northern region remained intact by virtue of its perceived
homogeneity. This division was made solely for administrative
convenience of Britain and not towards Nigeria's national unity. So,
when the 1947 Constitution was revised in 1951, it signalled the
beginning of the decolonization of Nigeria. In 1954, Nigeria became
a federation with self–governing status granted to Eastern and Western
regions in 1957 and to Northern regions in 1959. This arrangement was
followed by the 1960 Constitution which Nigeria obtained Independence
from Britain on October 1, 1960. Hence, until 1963, Nigeria inherited
Enugu, Ibadan and Kaduna as the Eastern, Western and Northern
regional administrative headquarters respectively, with Lagos as the

federal capital. In 1963, the midwestern region was created with its capital in Benin City.

For generations to come, the aftermath of European and Arab invasion of Nigeria as well as their influence shall be remembered as one of the most notorious episodes of its early development. The fission and fusion of territories have since produced nothing but an epileptic nation--from the prophetic cultural pollution as depicted in Chinua Achebe's (1959) *Things Fall Apart* to his *No Longer at Ease*. The British final departure from Nigeria heralded not only an impossibility of solving the problem of Nigeria's ethnic diversity but also its apocalyptic destruction as a unified nation–state. But the current instability in Nigeria should not come as a total surprise. It is noteworthy that "the Colonial administration in Nigeria was at no point designed to produce a united nation–state. Diverse people were brought together under a common umbrella of British rule" (National Youth Service Corps 1973, 80).

NIGERIA:
REGIONAL GOVERNMENT AND CAPITAL CITIES
BETWEEN 1955 AND 1967

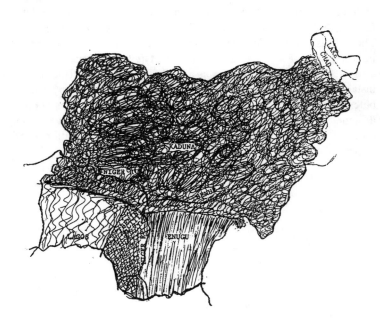

KEY

    Northern Region (Kaduna)

    Midwestern Region (Benincity)

    Western Region (Lagos)

    Eastern Region (Enugu)

Chapter Five

Nigerians and Their Historical Origin

There are no people without a history. To think otherwise is to think of a person without a name, origin or society. Krech, Crutchfield and Ballachey (1962, 308) stated that:

> From birth to death man lives out his life as member of a society. And to live in a society is to be under constant, all–pervasive social influence. For the central characteristic of a society is that it is an organized collectivity of interacting people whose activities become centered around a set of common goals, and who tend to share common beliefs, attitudes and modes of action.

Historically, events about people, places and things are usually learned by reading written documents of eyewitnesses or by listening to elders. Other methods of learning history come by way of derived sources or through divine inspiration. Most biblical writings such as the book of Revelation are presumed to come by way of divine inspiration. Early African history is said to be handed down through story telling often regarded as a primitive method of preserving historical data in their pure form. In fact, there is an African belief that says that: "One can only get a pure African history from a fortune teller." Consequently, some indigenous historians have become rather cautious in reporting early African history. They tend to be afraid of writing or reporting what can be termed as "bad history," claiming that enough of bad history about Africa has already been written by most European writers. To African historians, it should be remembered that: "half bread is better than none." As it can be expected, written documents relating to the origin of the early people of Africa in general and Nigeria in particular are scarce, while the available ones are sketchy and inconclusive.

In general, the historical origin of man seems intricately connected to such historical sites as the Nile, the Old Sahara and the regions surrounding the Mediterranean Sea. Etiologically, these Mediterranean regions have remained significantly important in mapping early human life and civilization. The early history of the Egyptians who also called themselves Kam or Kam–Au meaning Black People or the Black God People is connected to the biblical account of Africans –Ham (Psalms 78:51; 105:23, 27; 106:21,22). Egypt is Kamit meaning the land of the Blacks. Also, Morse (1970) stated that in Psalms, Egypt is referred to several times as the "land of Ham; evidently because of this Biblical genealogy and the name of Egyptian deity, Ammon. . . (p. 4409). In much of the old testament, the name Africans, Egyptians, Ethiopians, Canaanites are used interchangeably.

Another important source to trace the history of Africans is the Biblical account relating to Noah and the flood. Even though, the overall biblical account of the flood and the children of Noah, namely Ham, Shem and Japheth, is somehow flawed in linking different races as descendants of the three children of Noah to deduce the children of Ham as Africans, it is successful in shedding some light on the theory of the origin of man. There is the misconception that Ham and his descendents were cursed, which relates to the current economic, social and politcal destitution now found in Africa. Such relationships have lacked a scientific credence. To clarify the misconception surrounding Ham and his so–called Curse, Felder (1993,ix) stated that:

> The "curse of Ham" is a post–biblical myth. In fact, the sons of Noah – Shem, Ham Japheth – do not represent three different races. (It is an absurdity of no small order to claim that Noah and his wife could produce offspring that would constitute three distinct racial types!) In Gen. 9:18–29, Ham is not the recipient of a curse. The text explicitly says, "Let Canaan be cursed." Furthermore, Ham does not mean "Black" in Hebrew; it translates literally as "hot" or "heated." It does not make sense to say, logically or scientifically, that within the ten generations of Adam to Noah (and without the introduction of any outside factors), a genetic change took place

which allowed one man (Noah) and his wife (of the same race as himself) to produce children who were racially different!

The name Edenites has received less publicity in much of the available literature due to the controversy of Eden and "its exact location" (Morse 1970, 2927). Nevertheless, the history of the garden of Eden (Adam and Eve) before the geological shift and the theory of human mutation have made more sense in tracing the origin of man on planet earth and his connection with Noah's flood. Conceptually, the name Edenites, meaning Africans, is supported by biblical evidence linking Adam and Eve, both Africans as the only ancestors of human kind. There is a great body of knowledge supporting the theory that in Biblical times African landscape extended to and included what is now known as the Middle East area where Jesus of Nazareth, called Christ, was born before his flight into a neighboring area – Egypt (see Holy Bible, Matt. 1:16–24;2:1–15).

The historical origin of the present day African is also connected with the history of North Africa migrational movement Southwards dating back to many centuries before Christ. This account is also consistent with man's early settlement in/around [Nigeria] West Africa as a whole. Davidson, Buah and Ajayi (1968,8) stated that:

Around 2000 B.C., there began a great natural change. The climate gradually became much drier. The Sahara received less and less rain. Its rivers began to fail. Little by little, its farming people had to move away and find new homes. Some went Northward and helped to form the Berber people of North Africa. Others pushed eastward to the margins of the fertile valley of the Nile. Others again came southward into West Africa.

Diop (1987, 213) added that:

The idea of a center of dispersal located approximately in the Nile Valley is worth considerations. In all likelihood, after the drying of the Sahara (7,000 B.C.), Black mankind first lived in bunches in the Nile Basin, before swarming out in successive spurts toward the interior of the continent.

In addition to improper chronology in the migrational account, there is yet another curiosity concerning the presence of native Africans inside Nigeria before the migrational movement. With this curiosity in

Noah's Family Tree: Biblical Account Of Race & Culture

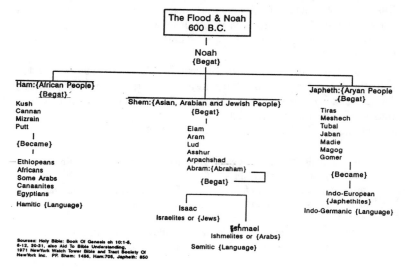

The Flood & Noah
600 B.C.

Noah
{Begat}

Ham:{African People}
{Begat}

Kush
Cannan
Mizrain
Putt

{Became}

Ethiopeans
Africans
Some Arabs
Canaanites
Egyptians

Hamitic {Language}

Shem:{Asian, Arabian and Jewish People}
{Begat}

Elam
Aram
Lud
Asshur
Arpachshad
Abram:{Abraham}

{Begat}

Isaac
Israelites or {Jews}

Ishmael
Ishmelites or {Arabs}

Semitic {Language}

Japheth:{Aryan People}
{Begat}

Tiras
Meshech
Tubal
Jaban
Madie
Magog
Gomer

{Became}

Indo-European
{Japhethites}

Indo-Germanic {Language}

Sources: Holy Bible: Book Of Genesis ch 10:1-5,
6-12, 20-31, also Aid To Bible Understanding,
1971 NewYork Watch Tower Bible and Tract Society Of
NewYork Inc. PP. Shem: 1486, Ham:705, Japheth: 850

mind, two theories have existed for examination. The first theory is that of the Edenites, beginning with the first African man and woman (Adam and Eve) to populate the earth. The second rather obscure theory is in connection with the Pygmies of Central African and other tribes who existed at different locations within prehistoric Africa. Anthropologically speaking, there are three main groups identified to have been present in Africa and had migrated Northwards to Nigeria's regions of West Africa. They were the Nilotic Negroes, Nigritians and the Negroes proper subraces. The Negroes proper subraces were classified and further grouped ethnologically into numerous tribes found in various parts of Western Africa. Most frequently mentioned in these groups is the Yoruba tribe.

The other Negro subraces were known in anthropology as the Pygmy Nigrillos, the "type sparsely distributed in equatorial Africa and the forest Negroes better known as the Bushmen who live in the S. African interior" (Morse 1970, 213). In essence, "the whole continent at that time was partially peopled by Pygmies...." (Diop 98, 212). Both Northward and Southward migrational movement were likely to affect the area now known as Nigeria relative to its population growth, lifestyle, intermarriages, trade, etc.

With special emphasis to the recent heterogenous population in Nigeria, the Niger River as well as its tributaries was regarded as an important factor to the early settlers as migration took place. Just as the Nile, the Niger provided life to the people who settled around it. The Niger River, the Benue River and the Delta regions did not only provide a source of livelihood for the early settlers, they also provided natural boundaries between them where their form of individualized identities, folkways, even dialects were developed. Though these boundaries separated one group from another, they nevertheless provided possibilities for neighborly agrarian coexistence between the North as a separate entity, and the entire South comprising of the Western and eastern settlements. It is important to point out that in today's Africa, rivers and streams have continued to provide natural boundaries between villages and towns. These natural boundaries are as respected and acceptable today as they were many years ago.

AFRICA: MIGRATIONAL MOVEMENT AND RELIGIOUS INFILTRATION INTO NIGERIAN REGION AROUND 600 AD

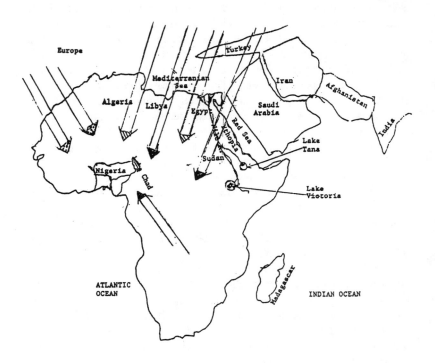

KEY

 Migrational Movement   7000–2000 BC

 Religion: Muslim Infiltration in 600s AD

 Religion: Christian Infiltration   15th–19th centuries

ETHNIC DEVELOPMENT

Eventually, Nigeria comprised of many ethnicities, towns and villages dotted over the entire piece of land surrounded to the North by early Niger settlers, to the east by Chad and Cameroon settlers, to the South by the Gulf of Guinea and to the West by Dahomey settlers. Most of these ethnic groups had different migrational history, historical origins and settlements. Consequently, Nigeria, became famous for its many independent ethnic kingdoms and empires. Ethnographically, the upper Niger and Benue Rivers namely the northmost lands comprised of different emirates and empires of the Tuaraq, the Berber, the Furah and lastly the Hausa who were conquered and usurped by the Furah around the 15th century. Conjointly, their religion was that of the Furah Mohamedanism, now known as Islam, while their Lingua Franca was the Hamitic language brought to them by the Northern immigrants.

Below the Niger and the Benue Rivers, however, was the southmost lands. Its settlers were predominantly the Yorubas, Ibos and the Cross River people sometimes referred to as the Cross River Ibos. The Yoruba occupied the southwestern part of the Niger River. Their early history is somehow obscure except that they are believed to be Sudanic immigrants who in the 18th century had formed a large empire which later disintegrated into petty kingdoms with distinct customs, laws and governments. Other writers like Cheikh Anta Diop and J. Olumide Lucas seem to agree that: "the Yoruba during antiquity lived in ancient Egypt before migrating to the Atlantic coast" and that similarity or identity of "language, religious beliefs, customs and names of persons, places and things" (Diop 1987,216) between the Yorubas and Egyptians have existed.

The Yorubas had always regarded the Ile Ife as the cradle of their "nations" owing their ancestry to Oduduwa whose kingdom spanned the areas we now call Benin Republic in the West, Ilorin in the North and some part of Bendal State, and whose children had also become rulers of other parts of the Yorubaland. While Ife remained the seat of many powerful rulers and Obas of Oduduwa ancestry, Oyo as well as Benin empire, flourished into political and cultural centers. Yoruba city states remained closely united under the spiritual and political leadership of Oni of Ife and Alaafin of Oyo respectively. They practiced traditional religion and had Yoruba as the lingua Franca of the entire Yoruba people.

Unlike the Yorubas, the Ibo, the Cross River Ibos and the Ogoja Ibos had always been different in their early associations. Their early form of government was "segmentary" in which families joined together with other families "in common loyalty to their founding ancestry. This loyalty is maintained by the group's religious beliefs, by their prayers at the shrines of their ancestors, and by their understanding of how their ancestors wished them to behave" (Davidson et al 1965, 114). Somehow democratic,

> most Ibos had governed themselves without giving much or any power to chiefs. Some however like those of Nri Awka towards the Niger, have had kings of their own; while the Cross River Ibo of the eastern Delta have made much use of the political associations such as Ekpe" (Davidson et al 1965, 113)

Trading and fishing were the main occupations of the Ibos of the central and Cross River regions respectively. On the lower southeastern region, there were prominent towns of the Cross River people such as Opobo, Calabar and the surrounding cities and villages. Their inhabitants were not Ibos, inspite of the use of the name Cross River Ibos and Ogoja Ibos. They were Efiks, Ibibios, Agojas and their neighbors. The names Cross Rover Ibos and Ogoja Ibos as used by most writers was an assumption that because of close physical resemblance, everyone in the Eastern region was an Ibo. Such generic use of the word "Ibo" for the entire area was likely to engender ethnic confusion. On the central eastern region, were prominent Ibo towns like Onitsha, Nsukka, Awka, and Warri while the delta regions had become trade centers and routes among the Ibos and the people of the salt waters –the Ndu Mili Nru.

INDIGENOUS RELIGION

Over the years, religion has played an important role in man's existence including the way he governs himself. In history, many wars have been fought on religious grounds and many persecutions have also taken place under the same pretext. The word Jihad is Arabic for holy war. The interplay of religion and politics first became preeminent in the Biblical times when Christ was confronted with the issue of taxation. "Render therefore unto Caesar the things which are Caesar's and unto God the things that are God's" (Matthew 22:21), he advised.

In Nigeria however, religion, is the "third force" in political group formation and identity, preceded by tribe and language. Much of the religious rivalry in Nigeria has been primarily between Islam and Christianity. In most parts of Nigeria, there is a comingling of religious, tribal and political values. To the contrary, most countries like the United States, in spite of the "religious freedom," has made a deliberate attempt to separate religion from politics usually called the "separation of church and state."

Valuation of religion tends to depend on which part of the world one is associated with. Accordingly, many well known forms of religion existing today include "Christianity, Hinduism, Buddhism, Confuciasm, Zoroastrianism, Judaism and Islam" (Mazrui 1986, 34), each having a different meaning and significance to those who practice it but ultimately connoting the importance of their union to God. Very seldom do most contemporary social scientist write meaningfully on religion which is indigenous to Africa. This code of silence can be attributed to three major factors.

First, African form of worship has been radically displaced to a trickle since the European and Arab invasion of Africa. For example, when we conducted the study in 1989 in the remotest part of Ibibioland in Nigeria, it was discovered shockingly that all participants in the study were Christians (See Umoren 1989,84). Item 6 on the study instrument was designed with the expected outcomes of some Christians, some Muslims, some traditional African religion worshippers and some others. This discovery also meant that different religions in Nigeria namely Islam and Christianity are still localized in the early strongholds of each invader.

In most cosmopolitan areas of an African society, religious practice is assorted, ranging from Muslims to Christians and to traditional religious groups. Generally, these religious groups would coexist only if the interest of their political group agenda is not threatened. The impact of religious diversity in Nigerian and in a generalized African social and political life was discussed in the preceding pages.

Second, assigning one name to African form of worship has been difficult due to the vastness of Africa and its diverse cultures, which perhaps had led to the erroneous conclusion that before African invasion in the 15th century, "the indigenous people of the continent had no well defined religion" (Morse, 1970. 213). In Africa, religion and culture were inseparable. Based on this conclusion, Europeans were encouraged to converge and to take advantage of Africa which was perceived as uncivilized.

Third, there has been consistent attempts to annihilate African religion and institute foreign religions. As recent as the 18th and 19th centuries there was a renewed upsurge of Christianity in Africa which resulted in some gains. In spite of their successes, Halford (1994, 9) warned that "Christianity is not yet an indigenous African religion. Historically two attempts to establish it failed. North Africa was extensively evangelized in the first six centuries of the Christian era. But Islam has all but eclipsed it."

In the 20th century, frequent clashes occuring in most African states between Christians and Muslims have been reported. These are usually clashes starting as a political struggle but having religious flavor and implications. The assumption is that when political control is achieved, religious domination can easily be achieved. But from an African point of view, it is troubling to recount the degree to which Africa has allowed the influence of foreign religion (Islam or Christianity) to destroy the fabric of African life.

Preserving native religious aspiration of Africa had not been an easy task upon the arrival of the invaders, to say the least. Some of the methods employed by native Africans to protect their religious initiatives and culture were no match to the carefully designed plan of the invaders to penetrate and occupy Africa. Physical resistence, even the militancy employed by Africans in some parts of Africa proved too little, too late. Most of their activities to repel colonialism were symbolic demonstrations, but nevertheless a useful signal that many African societies did not fully embrace colonialism. Typical among the militant resistance was the Mau Mau in Kenya which "fought the British as late as 1950s. . .the Mau Mau emergency in Kenya lasted from 1952–1960" (Mazrui 1986, 283-3).

Besides the human efforts to repel colonialism and its perpetrators, there was another problem that the Europeans had to face. This problem had something to do with the physical environment of Africa. To deal with the threat from mosquitoes, snakes, tse tse flies, indigenous religion, weather and general living conditions, Europeans and their Arab counterparts from across the Mediterranean adopted different approaches. Of all the above threats, indigenous religion seemed to have caused the invaders the most discomfort and insecurity due to its mysteriousness. Because religion is generally psychical, indigenous religion would have undermined the colonialist' program if it was not psychologically and physically dismantled.

In order for the European to thrive in this environment which according to them was in a "state of moral degradation" (Umoren 1989, 17), indigenous religion was first assaulted and defeated by converting the natives through relentless Bible and Koranic studies organized in churches, schools and mosques. To overcome the dangers from the physical environment, the Europeans wore footwears to protect them from snakes, and built mosquito nets to protect them from Tse Tse flies and mosquito bites. They had to clear the bushes and forests, and many times physically destroy important African shrines. The Arabs, who on the other hand had also been unfriendly with the European invaders, had to avoid the unfamiliar tropical condition by settling in the drier habitat which seems to explain the predominance of muslims in the northern Nigeria where they had occupied and maintained firm control ahead of the Europeans.

Throughout the period of European and Arab occupation of Nigeria,, proselytism was achieved by indoctrinating and brainwashing the natives unto the new ways of worship, and also by deliberately sabotaging native religions. Words such as "Juju" and "Gris Gris" were established and used by the Europeans to discredit all forms of indigenous worship. Juju was coined form the French "Joujou" meaning toy and French "Gris Gris" meaning charms (Parrinder 1978, 9). In every interpretation, a "toy" for instance is something without a substantial meaning or value – something which is worthless and charm means mere fascination.

Another point of controversy relative to the European perception of an indigenous religion was the concept of dualism as applied by Africans during worship. To most European philosophers such as Plato and Descartes, dualism meaning, composed of two parts –"being and non–being," and "mind and matter" respectively was well understood and accepted as an integral part of most religious practices and in understanding human nature. Morse (1970, 2882) stated that "dualism also has an ethical aspect namely, in the recognition of the independent and opposing principles of good and evil." Notwithstanding its critics, Africans had continued to adopt the concept of dualism in their form of worship. Most of its application relating to the principle of good and evil had a firm foundation before the arrival of Christianity and Mohamedanism.

Social norms, violation of social norms and punishment or reward thereof were based on the dualism, ie the separation of good from evil in the traditional African life. Africans also believed that behind every object they can see or touch, there was another object that they cannot see or touch. This belief had perhaps convinced most traditional Africans that it was efficacious to pray to their ancestral spirits and unto their Creator before inanimate objects. As we shall see, the use of images in religious worship was not limited to Africa, yet Africa was reprimanded for the use of images. The controversy should have been on the racial relevance of religious images that were imposed on Africans by some European church authorities. Indigenous form of worship including images as well as the JuJu and Gris Gris were misunderstood by the Europeans as idol worshipping. Africans had always been monotheistic in spite of their method of worship. For example, in Ibibioland of Nigeria a native doctor in performing his religious rites would first invoke the powers of *Abasi Onyong* (God Above) before invoking *Abasi Isong* (God Below), including the breaking of the *Kola* nut and libation and using his ancestors only as intercessors. The concept of "intercession" is not limited to African traditional religion. Other religions have successfully used it as well.

Even today, African religion still remains the most misunderstood and misquoted form of worship in the world. It is generally accepted that before the arrival of other forms of religion in Africa, Africans had their own forms and style of worship. Therefore the frequent notion that Africans were pagans or a bunch of irreligious people before the imposition of Christianity and Islam is fallacious and misguided. A religious individual is not necessarily a spiritual individual.

As most social scientists would agree, a human being is basically psychological and spiritual. Even so, colonial religious teaching in Africa was often off the mark by showing no consideration for an African's unconscious or introverted materials – his spiritual makeup. Carl Jung, a renowned psychologist and psychiatrist (1875–1961), saw an individual's unconscious as the undeveloped element of personality containing racial factors which we inherited from our ancestors. Religion without spiritualism is meaningless. African people of antiquity have been known to be both religious and spiritual in their form and style of worship. To them, a person's transcendentness in worship was not based on his outward religiosity but rather on his inward spiritualization. This behavior was best explained in the attitudes of the Pharisees on human self–righteousness (Luke 18:9–14).

Perhaps the misunderstanding and misquotation about African religion can be put to rest first by understanding what religion basically is and what it seeks to accomplish.

Funk and Wagnalls Standard College Dictionary (1963) defined religion as "the beliefs, attitudes, emotions, behavior etc. constituting a man's relationship with the powers and principles of the universe, especially with deity or deities. . . " (p. 1136). Merril (1969, 263) stated that the "the ultimate function of religion is to provide a meaning to life. . . religion also provides an organized culture pattern by which the individual can meet and it is hoped, surmount the crises of life."

One can also try to understand a particular religion through its "form" and "style." The form of religion implies its organizational set-up relative to its personnel and lines of authority while the style of religion implies the method of actual worshipping. Religious organizations that are bureaucratic and hierarchical in form are usually methodic, ritualized and rhythmic in style while others that are proprietary in form are usually spontaneous and participatory in style. This definition marks the fundamental difference between an imported religion and African religion.

Based on the given definition and intent of religion, Keesing (1976) has doubted the efficacy of today's organized religion in promoting man's much needed moral discipline. He stated that: "religion may govern people's moral conduct or be unconcerned with morality. Such variety makes a search for a common denominator frustrating and not very productive." (p. 386). Keesing's assessment did not only apply to Nigeria but throughout Africa as we ponder about what is wrong with Africa today. It also seemed to imply that organized religion may be failing in cleansing the "soul," controlling the "mind," and strengthening the "body." Today, our societies are confronted with the problem of rapid decay in moral leadership, uncontrollable killings, lack of respect for humanlife, political corruption, social conflict, economic uncertainties, and so on. Africa needs to re–evaluate itself in light of what has gone wrong that needs correction. Perhaps Mazrui (1986) was right when he suggested that "the ancestors of Africa are angry" (p. 11).

Before the penetration of Africa by the Europeans and Arabs, Africa was at peace with itself. It was an organized culture shaped by social norms. Its method of worship significantly provided Africans with meaning and identity, fear of God and a sense of distinguishing right and wrong. Religion was something more than the abstractedness of the present day organized form and style of worshiping. Mazrui (1986) summarized the notion of African religion before the European and Arab invasion of Africa. He stated that:

> Long before the religion of the Crescent or the religion of the Cross arrived on African continent, Africa was at worship, its sons and daughters were at prayer. Indigenous religions had a concept of divinity which was decentralized. God is not in heaven, or on the throne or necessarily in the shape of man. The concept which some indigenous eastern Africans call Jok is primarily the process of being in essence of universal power, which inheres in life as a force in its own right. In indigenous religion, man was not created in the image of God: nor must God be conceived in the image of man. The universe and the force of life are the manifestation of God. (p. 135)

What was an African religion before the arrival of the Koran and the Bible, and what was the impact of this religion on African way of life? Part of the answers to this question has already been given in Mazrui's statement above. Traditional African religion (TAR) was the form of religion in which an African, depending on his culture, related to his God through his ancestors and through a wide range of deities such as the Sun Deity, River Deity, even the Tree Deity all of which had religious relevance to an African way of life. The belief was that these deities, in addition to explaining the concept of God, they represented the handwork of the Creator of the universe and their manifestation to men. With this belief, Africa was in concert with the world regarding the idea of applying deities to intercede between man and the Creator of the universe.

In the history of many continents, varieties of deities such as Babylonian deities, Egyptian deities, Deities of Medo–Persia, Grecian Deities, Roman Deities, Cannite Deities and Assyrian Deities had existed serving in the same capacity and purpose as African Deities. According to Aid to Bible Understanding of 1971, it is stated that:

> The striking similarity readily observable when comparing the gods and goddesses of ancient people can hardly be attributed to chance. Concerning this, Colonel J. Barnier, in his book *The Worship of the Dead*, writes "not merely Egyptians, Chaldeans Phoenicians, Greeks and Roman, but also the Hindus, the Buddhists of China and Thibet, the Goths, Anglo–Saxons, Druids, Mexicans and Peruvians, the Aborigines of Australia and even the savages of the South Sea

Islands, must have derived their religious ideas from a common source and a common centre: Everywhere we find the most startling coincidences in rites ceremoniès, customs, tradition and in the names and relations of their respective gods and goddesses" (*p. 667).

By any standard, a meaningful religion is that which provides self–identity and self–worth to those who practice it. Within the context of TAR, religious relevance on African people is paramount. During TAR worship, Africans seemingly relate and become bonded to their ancestral spirit––to the same people who prior to their death were kins, well known and well respected in the community––their saints.

In the Chinese culture where Christianity and Islam have made little or no inroad, religion based on ancestor worship is acceptable. Accordingly, specific similarity existing between Chinese religion and Traditional African religion include the following beliefs that:

all living persons owe their fortunes or misfortunes to their ancestors...all departed ancestors like other gods and spirits have needs that are not different from those of the living... Departed ancestors continue as in life to assist their relatives in this world. (Seybolt 1983,66)

In this section it is concluded that in Nigeria, religious beliefs and practices are no longer limited to being the vehicle by which the body, mind and soul are connected to God. Since the European and Arab invasion of Africa, religious subcultures of Christianity, Islam and traditional African religion have become fierce competitors politically and socially. Each of these religious subcultures, very much demarcated by tribal lines except TAR, has also formed an additional basis for discrimination. It is not surprising that "the Civil War in Nigeria has also been popularly interpreted as a war between the Muslim North and the Christian South" (Howard 1986, 108).

INDIGENOUS LANGUAGE

The importance of speech and language in human socialization cannot be overemphasized. It can be considered as the primary medium of all human association and transaction as he communicates with others. Krech, Crutchfield and Ballachey (1962, 273) stated that: "Man is a talking animal. He has built a world of words and he lives in this world as he lives in a world of things and persons. . . he uses words as tools to control his own behavior and the behavior of other persons." Keesing (1976,146) stated that "it is language that allows human to transcend many of the limitations imposed by biology, to build cultural models of their world and transmit them across generations."

The history of speech and languages in general is usually long and perhaps inconclusive. Many theories in connection with why people speak different languages have existed which can be linked not only to prehistoric Africa but also to other parts of the world as we know them today. The oldest and well known theory is that related to the Biblical account of the Divine Ordinance such as the creation of different "tongues" at the Tower of Babel (see Genesis 11:1–9). In recent years however, students of languages have viewed speech and languages as the product of evolutional origin and development.

Accordingly, every principal region of the world and state has its own dominant language. A dominant language may be referred to as the traditional or ethnic language of the original culture. In addition to the dominant language, most people today speak such languages as English, Spanish, French, Arabic, Swahili and Russian as a second language. In post colonial Africa, the second language is usually the language of its colonizers which initially competed with the native tongue as a subculture. Parmelee (1994, A1) stated that "there are about 50 major languages spoken in Africa and as many as 2,000 languages less widely spoken." With specific emphasis to Nigeria, English and Arabic were each introduced as the languages of doing business and classroom instruction by the invaders. Traditionally, English as a second language (ESL) was introduced to the South of Nigeria while Arabic as a second language (ASL) was predominantly used in the North.

Most Africans today are bi–lingual, such as French speaking or English speaking Africans, etc. The second language of these Africans is the language of the colonial masters which failed to replace the native dialect, but nevertheless continued to play an important role in African interethnic relation and communication. These linguistic allegiances have also been seen as an additional contributing factor to ethnic diversity in most African societies. In Nigeria, the issue of language diversity inter alia has produced many debates among "those whose responsibility is to forge a true Nigerian nation." (National Youth Service Corps, 1973, 65).

Today, the psycho–sociological impact of a multi–language society is becoming much more acute in Nigeria as in many other African societies. Generally, people who speak the same language tend to view themselves as conversationally close and belonging to the same culture. On the contrary, those who do not speak the intragroup language are usually considered as "outsiders" whose interests are different and perhaps unimportant. It is also noteworthy that in most multi–ethnic societies, a language difference between a dominative group and a marginalized one tends to encourage and reinforce a psychological oppression of one ethnic group by another. In Nigeria, this situation was most prevalent under the regional government when more than one ethnic group were artificially proximated.

Interpersonal rejection based on language culture may lead to a negative countergroup solidarity based on fear of the unknown. A few of the ethnic groups having their own distinct dialect and identity in Nigeria, but are socio–politically related, include the Igalas, Tivs, Hausas, Bornus, Yorubas, Edos, Ijaws, Igbos, Ibibios, and Efiks (see National Youth Service Corps). Tribal languages in Nigeria should not be abandoned, even though such suggestions had existed in the past. Such an abandonment may infringe on individual's rights and freedom. Language differences which are poorly managed can put a serious strain on national integration. By accepting such a premise, citizens should freely exercise caution in their use of language around others who may not speak the same language but have shared interests and goals. Nigeria has multiplicity of dialects. Even though English language has become the language of official business and classroom instruction, the existence of these dialectic differences between ethnic groups has been an obstacle to Nigeria's integration as a nation.

Chapter Six

Ethnicity as Obstacle
To Nigeria's National Unity

In the previous chapter, the definitions of ethnicity and tribe were given for the purpose of distinguishing one from the other. In some instances however, these two terms have been used interchangeably. We shall not make any bones concerning their differences even though the term "tribe" is more applicable to Africa. In Nigeria, over 200 different tribal groups can be identified. Some of these tribal groups are radically different socio-culturally from one another based on years of weakened ancestral connection, lack of early association, foreign intervention, and economic and educational disparities between the tribal groups. These set of circumstances has been problematic in achieving national cohesiveness and paving the road to national integration. This problem was noticed by Grove Haines much earlier when he pointed out that:

> "the size of Nigeria and the accident of history have made it more difficult for a sense of nationhood to develop there. The Northern and Southern parts of the colony have different tribes' culture and religion (Haines 1955,295).

For a long time, Nigeria was perceived to comprise of three tribes, Yoruba, Hausa and Ibo. This misinformation which failed to account for other diverse tribes had remained so until 1967 and also led to the unsuccessful politico–administrative regionalization of Nigeria into North, West and East. Many historians have also pointed out that with the regional experimentation itself, the regional lines demarcating North, West and East should have been on the natural waterways of the Niger and the Benue Rivers adjoining the delta rivers to the South. Instead, the artificial lines created by Lugard were followed which further caused the dispersion of people of common heritage. When the Northern boundaries were extended southwards beyond these rivers in relation to the 1900 Lokoja episode, an important African tradition was violated. This violation has undoubtedly contributed in part to the socio–political problem of the post–colonial Nigeria such as the current Middle Belt struggle for political self–determination.

When a fourth region, the Midwest, was carved out the western region in 1963, more questions should have been raised concerning the wisdom of separating people of the same ancestry. It is noteworthy that the Midwesterners and the Westerners are believed to be of the same Yoruba ancestry. They are both descendants of Oduduwa. Oba of Benin is said to be the grandchild of Oduduwa, whose father was Alaafin of Ojo. In the first place, the creation of the western region which included midwest was originally based on tribal affiliations of that entire region. This is an example of the concept of the "fission" and "fussion" of tribes which have been ongoing in Nigeria and has accomplished nothing. Most political scientists have long argued that regionalization as a means of preserving Nigeria more than any thing else provided the basis its future disintegration.

Primarily, regionalization, except in the Yoruba land, had huge problems by failing to take into account the significance of language differences, customs and lifestyles of many of the in–between tribal groups in the regions. As a result many tribes were marginalized into minority status within the larger tribal groups – the region. For example, in the regionalization formula any person who came from anywhere in the Eastern region was automatically regarded as an Ibo. In much the same way, all Westerners were only Yorubas and all Northerners were Hausas.

The perception of only three [main] tribes, namely Yoruba, Hausa and the Ibo, in Nigeria has lingered till today leading to the so called 1990s *"Wa–So–Bia."* So for many decades, Nigeria's political and social scenes have been dominated by them, leaving the other tribal groups to play second fiddle. "Wa" in Yoruba, "So" in Hausa and "Bia"

ERA OF POLITICAL DYSFUNCTIONALITY

DATES   EVENTS

1959   Election

October   Independence and 1st Republic
1960   Nnamdi Azikiwe–Monarchial President
                         Abubakar T. Balewa–Federal Prime Minister
                         Ahmadu Bello–Northern Premier
                         Obefami Awolowo–Western Premier
                         Michael Okpara–Eastern Premier

(1951) –   Formation of Major Tribal Political Parties
1962   NPC – Northern Political Party
                         Action Group – Western Political Party
                         NCNC – Eastern Political Party
                         NEPU – Northern Element Progressive Party:
                             Northern Political Party
                         UMBC – United Middle Belt Congress

May 1962   Federal Election
                         Coalition NCNC + NPC = United Peoples
                     Grand Alliance (UPGA)
                         Problem in Western Region
                         Federal State of Emergency
                         6 Year Development Plan – 1962–68
                         Action group leader charged with treason

January   Akintola headed Western House of Assembly
1963   suppported by the Federal Gvoernment
                     Midwest became a separate region
                     Awolowo imprisoned for treason
                     Prime Minister Sir Abubakar Tafawa Balewa
                         announced Nigeria's population of 56 million
                     Nigeria attained a Republican status
                     Dr. Azikiwe became a ceremonial president of the
                         Federation Nigeria

June 1964   General strike for failure of federal government to
                   implement work wage recommendation

Dec–Jan   Federal election crisis
1965   NPC and its allies won the election
                   President Azikiwe reluctantly swore in Abubakar as
                   Prime Minister

October   Western Election
1965   Election Crisis
                   Akintola's faction once again was victorious
                   Action Group protested
                   Anti–riot police and Army deployed to restore order
                   to Western Nigeria supported by Prime
                   Minister

January   Mutiny in the Armed Forces led by Nzeogwu
1966   Western Premier Akintola, killed
                   Northern Premier Ahamadu Bello, killed
                   Prime Minister Abubakar, killed
                   Minister of Finance Okotieboh, killed
                   Eastern Premier Opara under house arrest
                   Midwest Premier Osadebey under house arrest
                   President Azikiwe out of the country for medical
                   reasons

1966   Military rule headed by Gen. Ironsi overthrew of
                   the First Republic

January   Decree No. 1 (Suspension of the Constitution)
1966   Formation of military government with 4 governors:
                   Lt. Col. Ojukwu – East
                   Lt. Col. Adekunle Fajuyi – West
                   Lt. Col. Ejoor – Midwest
                   Lt. Col. Hassan Katsina – North

March 1966   Massacre of Ibo in the North

May 1966   Decree No. 34 (Unitary Republic)

July 1966	Counter Coup by Lt. Col. Danjuma Gen. Ironsi killed Lt. Col. Fajuyi killed (Replaced by Col. Adebayo) Major Nzeogwu killed (fighting)

July 1966	Brigadier Ogundipe in charge
	–refused to repeal Decree No. 34
	   –Lt. Col Gowon taken prisoner by dessident soldiers; later released
	   –Lt. Col. Gowon asked by dissident soldier to take part in negotiation as Commander in Chief

August 1966	Lt. Col Gowon is Commander in Chief Lt. Col Ojukwu opposition to Lt. Col. Gowon Political detainees released (Awolowo, Enahoro and Okpara) Abolition of Decree No. 34 and Reinstatemtent of Nigeria as a federation by Gowon
August 1966	Killing of the Northerners at Enugu, Owerri, Port Harcourt and Onitsha
September 1966	Ad hoc constitutional conference Proposals for states North proposed "automonous" states West proposed 18 states with strong central gov't Midwest proposed 12 states with weak central gov't Lagos proposed multistate federal structure East proposed a union of four virtually independent regions North change its former position Conference adjournment for independent celebration
October 1966	Adhoc constitutional conference reconvened East boycott of the subsequent conferences
November 1966	Conference adjourned indefinitely

November 1966	Ojukwu's policy speech (Easterners could not live in Nigeria)
January 1967	Aburi Conference Aburi result agreed by 5 Military leaders (Decree No. 8) Gowon refused to implement Aburi's decision on legal and economic reasons
January 1967	Gowon's statement in Lagos on Aburi Accord Ojukwu's statement in Port Harcourt on Aburi Accord Hassan Katsina met with Northern Emirs on Aburi derived policy
March 1967	Ojukwu declared East a disturbed area
March 1967	Supreme Military Council met Ojukwu did not attend
May 1967	Gowon declared state of emergency (Decree No. 14) throughout Nigeria; abolished 4 regions and created 12 states Ojukwu is mandated to secede Gowon declared himself the Dictator of Nigeria
May 1967	East declared Republic of Biafra
June 1967	Chiefs of Armed Services met at Lagos. Hassan Katsina attended with two governors from the Northern states.
June 1967	Gowon released a code of conduct for his troops
July 1967	Civil War started
January 1970	Civil War ended

July 1975	Bloodless coup d'etat Gowon overthrown by Gen.Murtala Muhammed, continued with the state of emergency
January 1976	Murtala Muhammed assassinated Obasanjo enthroned as Commander in Chief
September 1978	Ended state of emergency Ban lifted on former political activities
November 1979	Formulation of political parties Birth of Second Republic Shagari elected president
December 1983	Bloodless Coup d'etat led by Gen. Buhari Death of 2nd Republic Buhari became Commander in Chief of the Supreme Military Council (SMC) Buhari enacted laws that could not be challenged by the courts
August 1985	Bloodless coup d'etat led by Gen. Babangida Gen. Babangida became Commander in Chief of the Armed Forces Ruling Council (AFRC)

March 1987	Clash between Muslims and Christians at
	    Kafanchan.
	Formation of Advisory Council on Religious Affairs
	    (ACRA) by Gen. Babangida

November 1988	Muslims' demand for inclusion of Shari'a Court in the Nigerian Constitution. Debates and ACRA banned.
March 1989	Formation of National Electoral Commission (NEC) Formation of Political Parties with the National Republican Convention NRC and the Social Democratic Party SDP as Finalists.

May 1990   Local election held and political institution
                  established at state and local levels of
                  government

April 1990   Seizure of Federal Radio station at Kaduna and an
                  attack on Presidential Residence in an
                  attempted Coup d'etat by Maj. Gidion Orkar

December   Federal Capital was moved from Lagos to Abuja
1991

September   Presidential primaries held
1992

October   Result of Presidential primary election suspended
1992

November   Presidential election postponed to June 12, 1993 by
1992   Babangida.
                  All candidates for September's Presidential
                      primaries disqualified.

January   AFRC was replaced by National Defense and
1993   Security Council (NDSC)

June 1993   Federal (Presidential) election held
                  Abiola elected President

July 1993   Gen. Babangida annulled election result

August 1993   Gen. Babangida forced out of office
                  Gen. Babangida appoint Mr. Shonekan as head of
                      Interim Civilian Administration

November   Gen. Abacha dismissed Shonekan by force
1993   Gen. Abacha became Commander in Chief of
                  AFRC

in Ibo means come or come t(
The anticipated coalition by
trigger minority organization
Nigeria.

Beside marginalizing (
others, regionalization formu
produced many opportunists
posed by the adversities o
indigenous leaders were po
Nigeria did not take into c
tribesmen who had felt that
regions which they were a

Democracy 104 Awolowo as a betray regions. Fear of national wealth maneuvering feud invol- Awolow outco the

DEATH OF THE REPUBLIC

At the end of the de jure colonial rule in Nigeria in 1960, the problem of ethnicity and tribalism were left in tact and unresolved. Throughout the first and second Republics and what was to the the third Republic in 1993, Nigeria continued to find itself in many political predicaments. Independence for Nigeria was like a trap that a hunter sets for his prey. There were no political mechanism in place to galvanize different tribal groups or to strengthen the loose center in Lagos. For the colonialists, a weak center was necessary if the policy of indirect rule was to succeed. In much the same vein, indigenous Nigerian politicians tended to favor the Divide and Rule policies of tribal kingship. The failure to recognize, prioritize and tackle from the onset of independence the problem of tribal diversity relative to national unity, meant that political collapse beginning with the First Republic was imminent.

The first step to self governing after 1960 was the formation of political parties. Three major parties were formed –the National Council of Nigerian Citizens (NCNC), the Northern People's Congress (NPC) and the Action Group (AG). These political parties "were based on regionalism or tribalism or both, with each party solidly supported by its region's dominant ethnic group –the NPC by the Hausa–Fulani, the NCNC by the Ibo, and the Action Group by the Yorubas." (National Youth Service Corps, 1973, 158).

Accordingly, the ill–fated mergence between NCNC and NPC was immediately perceived by the Western Action Group, headed by Chief

y political conspiracy by Northern and Eastern
ɔmination and disproportionate distribution of
ɔ pre−eminent in the West. Meanwhile, the political
the West itself did not help matters. It was the family
ɩg the federal opposition and Action Group leader, Chief
and his deputy premier Chief Samuel Akintola and the
ɔe of the 1962 census, that brought things to a head resulting in
ɩrst military takeover and the killing of the Northern and Western
ɔlitical leaders in 1966.

One point about regionalization that needs to be explored is the political illusion and ambition it generated. Because each region was large enough at least in comparison to most states in Africa, it was not unthinkable that making the regions into independent states were generally considered by most ambitious regional leaders. During the ad−hoc constitutional conference of 1966, following the breakdown of Ironsi's regime, regional memorandums were presented by the regional delegates who, except Midwest, advocated a confederation of four "regions with each region having the "right to secede completely and unilaterally. . . in which each region could secede whenever it so desired" (National Youth Service Corps 1973, 159).

Between September 1966 and March 1967, Nigeria faced a political uncertainty, followed by an indefinite adjournment of that constitutional conference. There were also rumors of secessions. In March of 1967, Chief Awolowo was quoted as saying that: "were the East to secede from the federation, the West (including Lagos) would also follow suit and proclaim its sovereignty" (p. 161). The feasibility of secession noted therein perhaps had a lot to do with the creation of the historic Republic of Biafra by Ojukwu on May 30, 1967 in these resounding words: "Fellow countrymen and women, you the people of Eastern Nigeria. . . long live the Republic of Biafra" (Kirk−Green, 1967, 451−53). Ojukwu's action supposedly mandated by the eastern chiefs and elders was counteracted by Gowon's steadfastness on one Nigeria.

On November 30, 1966, he issued a statement which read in part as follows: "Fellow countrymen, I wish to speak to you this evening about the measures which the federal military government will implement to save the country form disintegrating" (Kirk−Green 1971, 306). It was from then on that the slogan "to keep Nigeria one is a task that must be done" became associated with Gowon's administration, a goal which he and many of his successors have so far failed to accomplish. There were as many unanswered questions then as there are now whether or not the goal of keeping Nigeria one was to satisfy the needs of a particular ethnic group or the nation as a whole. There were many people especially the Easterners, who had felt that because of the pre-eminence tribal interest in Nigeria, such a goal could not possibly be in the interest of a unified Nigeria.

Following the infamous Northern massacre of the Easterners and the failed Aburi Accord, Ojukwu claimed that Easterners [as a tribe] had no place in Nigeria. Gowon saw things differently. Every tribe including the Ibos belonged in the Federation, he maintained. Most scholars have however viewed tribal struggle in Nigeria predominantly as a struggle to maintain control of natural resources perpetrated by tribalism. One of these natural resources was the "eastern crude oil" which in essence had to be protected from the rest of Nigeria but saved for Biafra. Even though both sides of the civil war had oil at stake, nothing was said openly about its importance as the cause of the Civil War. All the ambitions or fears by the Northerners or Easterners were buried in the nationalistic rhetoric and the killings that took place before the war while the Westerners sat on the fence. One must not forget that these events took place at the time when the North had considered itself as underprivileged economically and educationally. The merits of this assertion should be considered very carefully.

To this point, it was apparently obvious that Gowon's goal was dead in terms of becoming a reality but very much alive in rhetoric; and Nigeria had entered into a brutal, ill-considered Civil War which still failed to produce unity in Nigeria after it ended in 1972. At the end of the Civil War, Nigeria was left as fragile as ever socio-politically while its economic life hanged on a balance. As we stated earlier, Nigeria's social, economic and political problems do not occur because the country is not wealthy. In fact Nigeria may be too wealthy for its own good. The problem has existed because using natural resources as a bait, many ethnic groups have demanded their autonomy in order to control these resources.   The creation of states in Nigeria in 1967 [still ongoing], like the regionalization policy had similar political and economic goals for ethnic autonomies.

It was in 1947 that the first ethnic group consciousness started, coinciding with the Richards Constitution. The first ethnic organization was the Ibibio Union followed by others such as the Ibo Union, Edo Union, Ijaw Progressive Union, the Calabar Improvement League, the Egbe Omo Oduduwa. Recommendation for early agitation for ethnic group self–determination and cultural sovereignty as contained in the 1937 book *The Political Blueprint of Nigeria* by Dr. Nnamdi Azikiwe and in *The Path to Nigerian Freedom* by Chief Obafemi Awolowo were ignored by the Richard's Constitution in lieu of the tripatite regional government. History also has it that the idea of the creation of states as a gateway to national unity was first conceived in the 1950's. It must be remembered that from the onset, Nigeria lacked political direction toward detribalization. The mixed feelings between detribalization and tribalization for national unity has always been noted throughout Nigeria's political culture. Every attempt to manage Nigeria depended on either the fusion or fission of different parts of Nigeria based on linguistic, ethnic or cultural affinity aimed at group compatibility.

Following the 1951 movement to create the Midwest state, the Western House of Assembly passed a resolution supporting the creation of the Western state while in 1953, the newly formed Middle Belt Peoples Party demanded a separate state for the Middle Belt. Likewise in the East, the COR state movement was in high gear for Calabar, Ogoja and Rivers people. In the North, it was Aminu Kanu who began the Northern movement to demand for Kano state. Between 1957 and 1960, numerous discussions about minority right to self determination were undertaken at different quarters. This demand was temporarily silenced. According to Britain, the creation of states at that time would have delayed Nigerian independence for two more years beyond 1960. However, the creation of the Midwest region in 1963 reopened new appeal for the creation of states in the North and East.

Following the dark days of the late 1960s, and shortly before the civil war, policymakers under the direction of General Gowon summarily believed that if the nation was further fragmented into twelve states using the provincial guidelines, the problem of ethnicity would be solved. We have since observed that regionalization, provincialization, and even the creation of new additional states, though a welcomed development, are equally frail and short of meeting Nigeria's political goals for unity. Quite recently, there is some misgiving concerning the number of states that must be created to stop further agitation for new ones. There seems to be no clearly defined criteria in this regard. Some predictions suggest that until every village or tribe becomes a state, agitations for new states can be expected. We believe that even though the concept of states tends to have the promise of approximating Nigerians by their ethnic roots and thereby creating a natural cohesiveness within the tribe, it should be based on the concept of national political unity and administrative efficiency considerations. National unity depends on effective central government and not just on the fragmentation of the nation to satisfy tribal needs for statehood. The survivability of individual states as well as the capability of all Nigerians to live together is vitally important. While rural development is inherent in state creation, the political survival of the nation is important. These two issues must remain balanced, and the problem of tribalism must be minimized.

In most Third World countries, like Nigeria, there are two types of tribalism. They are civilian tribalism and military tribalism. Civilian tribalism is the prejudices and conflicts between two or more tribal groups in a multi–ethnic society. Military tribalism is the support systems shared between the military and the ruling class of the same tribe for the purpose of power domination. In Africa, it has become rather popular that the civilian dictatorship is covertly backed by the military loyalists while a military dictatorship, as a matter of convention, is backed by its civilian ruling class. This new system of governing has made African dictators very formidable. Some of these dictators have already demonstrated the arrogance of declaring themselves not only presidents but also presidents for life inspite of public outcry, political protest, even civil disobedience. There is a basic principle of government which supports the conventional wisdom that he who controls the arms and the currency will control the borders. The control of borders implies the enslavement of citizens into a territory where their human rights are abused.

An example of a closed society is a communist state where the currency, arms and borders are usually controlled by the state. In Nigeria, as in the rest of Africa, the concept of power control is inherent in tribal politics. Tribal politics is often developed when the military dictatorship and the ruling class of the same tribe are backing each other. This unfortunate development in African politics is the reason for the diminished national consciousness which has made the development of a national political system an uphill battle. To develop the potential for national polity, the right political consciousness must be developed. Such consciousness must be nationalistic rather than tribalistic. Tribal consciousness should only serve as a grassroot for national consciousness.

NIGERIA: 30 State Governments and Their Capital Cities
1967 – 1994

#	state capitol
*	state name
‡	federal capitol

Chapter Seven

Road to Democracy
and National Unity

In approaching the subject of Nigeria's democracy and political
unity, we are mindful of the fact that since Independence in 1960,
Nigeria has lacked real peaceful intertribal coexistence. Intertribal
mistrust is perceived by most people inside and outside Nigeria to cause
not only national disloyalty by member tribes but also the prolonged
lack of national political stability and economic development. In
Nigeria, tribal cold war began where the Civil War left off. There can
be many theories allegedly responsible for this national tragedy. Be that
as it may, due to the degree of the economic backwardness the nation
is now facing, any factor contributing to such backwardness--a person,
place or thing is unacceptable. There are provoking questions that all
Nigerians must succinctly and truthfully answer about their continuous
coexistence.

The main questions that need answering in this regard are as
follows:

1) Are Nigeria's social and political problems resolvable?
2) Is Nigeria capable of achieving national unity through
   democratic means?
3) Does a lasting solution to Nigeria's 35-year old social, political
   and economic malady lie in its disintegration?

When Gen. Abacha's Constitutional Conference was due to start on the 27th of June 1994 at Abuya, its original goal was to examine these pertinent questions and its membership was to the rank and file Nigerians and not politicans. According to an open letter to the President of the United States, Bill Clinton, by Chief Egwuonwu U. Kalu which was published in *The Washington Post* of Thursday, October 27, 1994 and dated October 1, 1994, 63 familiar names in Nigerian politics were listed as conference signatories. In this letter, it was maintained that "the ultimate aim of the conference is to lay a sound foundation for early return to constitutional democratic rule...among the delegates are former chief actors in the last democratically elected government of the 1st, 2nd and 3rd Republics." (p. A28). But since that announcement, there was what Bakare (1994, A1) described as: "a parade of inconsistencies --Diya, Abacha, Gana, Onagoruwa," calling the goals of the conference a "record of contradictions."

The lack of conference focus on the part of the military leaders was also raised, all of which seemed to force many Nigerians to hold their breath in aimless expectation. Like the previous constitutional conferences (already too many), it was quite conceivable how solutions to the basic problems facing Nigeria could be disingenuously averted. It always seemed that Nigerians --these delegates have no moral courage to face the truth about the nation's mishaps and what to do about them. With this backdrop, Gen. Abacha's call for another Constitutional Conference lacked credibility and was greeted with suspicion by the public. The Conference seemed to offer the people no freedom of choice or alternative in the matter. Adigun Agbaje in his article entitled: *Beyond the General: Twilight of Democracy in Nigeria* stated:

> Critics insist that what Nigeria needs is not a constitutional conference – the 1989 constitution written during the Babangida era has not been tried – but a sovereign national conference where Nigerians could debate and negotiate new terms of union (Agbaje 1994,4).

Self–denial is a form of a defense mechanism which has its place in human behavior and personality, yet can be very harmful if it is overdosed. For too long, Nigeria leaders have failed to play an effective role in society by neglecting to make hard and right decisions either through denial, ineptitude or blatant avoidance of vital social and political issues. The political events which climaxed in 1994 and ended General Babaginda's regime were clear indications that Nigeria was living on borrowed time as far as confronting forthrightly issues of national unity and democracy. In the words of President James Buchanan of the United States, we likewise maintain that:

> Our union is a state of such inestimable value as to demand our constant and watchful vigilance for its preservation. In this view, let me implore my countrymen, North and South, to cultivate the ancient feelings of mutual forebearance and good will toward each other and strive to alley the demon spirit of sectional hatred and strife now alive in the land *(Mess. to Congress, Dec. 19, 1859)*.

In Nigeria, there are huge social, political and economic problems which the nation must solve. It is impossible for Nigeria to solve its economic problems without first of all cleaning up its social ills and putting its political house in order. It is simply fair to say that Nigeria has had enough setbacks in its socio–political even economic development. Because of tribal division, its citizens have continued to suffer in the "land of plenty" due to unnurtured social and economic conditions.

To obtain national integration and prosperity in Nigeria, OA Sanda in *Lectures on The Sociology of Development* has advocated that youths, students, labor and trade unions actively participate in different levels of the national decision making process, recommending that "inter–state and interethnic mobility are likely to produce intergroup marriages and criss–cutting of interest" (Sanda, 1992, 65). Specifically he stated that:

> Any genuine attempt to eradicate numerous micro–loyalties and re-orient the multi–ethnic society into manifesting a national identity and outlook will require not only the pursuit of those goals through formal means but also the encouragement of unity through indirect approaches. The extent to which the leadership succeeds in ensuring collective attachment and commitment to the nations will determine the level of integration attainable in the society. By the same logic, the level of integration established will significantly affect the nature, types and pace of development. This is why it is necessary to ensure that factors of ethnicity, leadership problems, political factionalism, language heterogeneity, and distributive injustice must be removed since they constitute obstacles to higher levels of integration and development. (Sanda 1992, 65–66).

History is full of the story of the rise and fall of great nations and empires. Some of these examples are Egypt and the Egyptian empire, Babylon and Babylonian Empire, Macedonia and the Macedonian Empire, Greece and Greek Empire, Rome and Roman Empire. In most of the African history, we have often read of the greatness of Ethiopia, Egypt and a few other nations and empires of the central and western Africa. The history of Nigeria in this regard tends to be the story of a nation that never rose but deteriorated. It is here that statement in the Washington Post describing "Africa...as a lost cause" is pertinent (Okie 1994, A29).

Over the years, many nations through their leaders have solved their national problems in various different ways. Nigeria cannot be an exception to the rule. For example, with regards to crime problem and the passage of the Crime Bill in the United States, President Bill Clinton on August 15, 1994 pleaded with the Congress, reminding them that "what we do here is not about us, it is about the rest of America." On July 1, 1957, Mao Tse-Tung of China warned the Chinese communists against what he called "a doctrinaire attitude: transplanting everything whether suited or not to the conditions of our country. This is not a good attitude" (Fremantle 1962, 296). Mao was an insightful nationalist who strived to liberate his people from the oppressive powers of elitism in society. His nationalist view centered mainly on people's revolution and comradeship considered to be beneficial to the Chinese people as a whole.

Like Mao, Paulo Friere advocated self-liberation through educational means. He believed that "men are not imprisoned within a permanent today, they emerge, and become temporized...as men relate to the world by responding to the challenges of the environment, they begin to dynamize, to master and humanize reality" (Freire 1973, 4). Freire's doctrine of rejecting human problems as a way of life has received much acclaim throughout the world. Some of the problems that Friere would advise Nigerians to solve are those relating to political instability, poverty, corrupton and greed, economic and educational inequalities, tribal prejudices and injustice, tribalism and so on.

In much the same vein, the Khit-Pen concept which was based on the Buddhist philosophy was adopted as the cornerstone of Thailand's social liberation. The basic premise of Khit-Pen was threefold:

> First, life is suffering; second, this suffering can be cured; third, in
> order to cure this suffering, the origin of the suffering must be

identified; only, then can those who seek solutions choose the right way or ways that will alleviate the suffering of the people (Srinivasan 1983, 27).

Ross (1955) saw the art of community building as resting on two important factors namely the "planning" and "community integration." During the process of planning, an effective identification of the problem is suggested. Community integration is defined "as a process in which the exercise of cooperative and collaborative attitudes and practices leads to 1) identification with the community, 2)interest and participation in the affairs of the community and 3) sharing common values and means for expressing those values" (p. 51). Like Ross, we advocate "diversity within unity" (p. 22) if Nigeria is to survive politically as a nation. To illustrate what we mean, we do not expect a Hausa man, a Yorubaman, or an Ibibioman to dress alike, think alike or eat the same kind of food or worship in the same manner etc. Rather, the overriding emphasis is on the amount of community feeling and involvement that create national unity. Nigerians' obvious lack of sense of community at a national level has remained its biggest dilemma. Harris (1972, 259) stated that "having achieved independence, African leaders and their followers faced a complex task of establishing a national identity as a basis for national unity. . . all African government sought to balance ethnic loyalty with emphasis on national identity."

Over the years, many unsuccessful attempts have been made to move Nigeria from the bondage of tribalism and de facto segregation to national unity and democracy, from today's human suffering to tomorrow's human prosperity. One of these unique attempts came in the 1970's shortly after the Civil War when General Gowon presented his "nine–point programme." These nine problem–solution areas were aimed at unifying and democratizing the nation. The program in our opinion seemed a good departure point to achieving the stated national objective. But, since October 1, 1970, the core problems relating to: 1) ethnic skewness in the military population, 2) corruption in Nigerian's national life 3) revenue allocation problems, and 4) lack of elections and installation of a popularly elected government in the center are still unresolved. These are the same chronic problems which General Gowon promised in vain to repair. Since then, many national leaders have failed in tackling these problems. The above problems are also recognized as representing obstacles which prevent Nigeria from achieving social harmony, democracy and economic prosperity.

Looking at Nigeria's problems from another angle, one can narrow them down and prioritized them as tribalism, greed and corruption, revenue sharing and lack of democratic ideals.

ISSUES OF TRIBALISM, LANGUAGE AND RELIGION

Tribalism is Nigeria's worst enemy today, pretense aside. To pretend that tribalism does not exist in Nigeria and that it is not causing more harm than good is a mistake which is likely to haunt Nigeria forever. Nigeria cannot survive as a nation unless the problems associated with tribalism are corrected. Tribalism retards the growth of a nation and poisons its moral conscience. Nkrumah in his *Class Struggle in Africa* called on Africans to denounce tribalism and stated that "many of the so-called tribal conflict in modern Africa are in reality class forces brought into conflict by the transition from colonialism to Neo-colonialism. Tribalism is the result, not the cause of underdevelopment" (Nkrumah, 1970,59).

The Nigerian bloody Civil War seemingly fought between the North and East in the late 1960's and early 1970's can be regarded as motivated by tribal hatred, mistrust, greed and not by nationalism, contrary to what most people were led to believe. Howard (1986, 940 saw "the Nigerian Civil War . . . as an example of tribalism in Africa." During American Civil War of 1861, Abraham Lincoln prayed: "We have highly resolved that these dead shall not have died in vain and this nation, under God shall have a new birth of freedom." It seems this same prayer which was answered in America was not answered in Nigeria. Why? It is tribalism. Unfortunately, neither do tribalistic practices in Nigeria indicate a declining trend nor are they limited to the controversial North and East of the civil war years. Nigerian tribalism exists in the smallest intertribal groups throughout the nation as well.

In essence, the fight to "keep Nigeria one" was not won. Defeating Nigerian tribalism does not need guns, killing, military decrees but economic and social development to liberate the masses from current levels of poverty. It needs higher consciousness of being, humanity, brotherhood, love and understanding for one another. The fact that after all these years Nigeria has not found the "root" to unity is unfortunate. The political stalmate that is caused by the military presence may be regarded as intentional, and in some fashion counterproductive to the nation's free-will to determine its fate. The retired Brigadier General David Mark (1993) in his *Newswatch* conversation referred to the military and pointed out that they've "realized sadly too that the solution to our economic and political problem could not be solved by simple military decree" (p. 12). The only criticism to General Mark's opinion is its timing.

Nevertheless, two important questions have arisen. Has the military lost its grace with the people in managing the country? What is at stake regarding the well–being of the country? These are not difficult questions. We do know, however, that Nigeria has not benefitted from the normal process of growing up politically. It is a normal [human behavior] for individuals or nations to develop amidst mistakes in order to reach new heights of maturity. The frequent interruption of democracy by military coups since 1967 has robbed Nigeria of this experiential opportunity, to the extent that politically and economically Nigeria is still in its infancy. David Mark's statement above could also imply that in Nigeria, government by military decree has lacked the continuity necessary for national development and detribalisation.

In the prewar and postwar periods, Nigerian leaders, military and civilian alike, had been found positioning themselves as tribal leaders. The Awolowist movement which was popularly perceived as a Yoruba tribal movement was also criticized by Gen. Olusegun Obasenjo in his book entitled *Not My Will*. For too long tribal tolerance has been a failure in Nigerian politics. Gen. Obasanjo summarized this situation when he described Awolowo as follows:

> My knowledge of Nigeria convinced me that whoever would lead Nigeria politically must be tolerant, accommodating and forgiving. Some of the antecedental actions of Chief Awolowo that I know had not convinced me that he had those commodities in sufficient quantities. (Obasanjo, 1990, 172).

In much the same vein, the Zikist movement was later found to be nothing but tribalism coated with rhetoric nationalism. Likewise, Hassanian doctrine of "North first" and Ojukwuism of East being "pushed out of Nigeria" of the mid 1960's did not in retrospect validate the spirit of national unity. Of all the five regional military governors in Gowon's administration, Cols. Hassan Katsina and Odumegwu Ojukwu were noted for their outspokenness in the events that precipitated the civil war. Unfortunately, some of these old tribal patriots are still around, either benefitting form their tribal stance or parading as converted political nationalists. In Nigeria, even disgraced politicians do not fade away; they always keep coming back, usually supported by their tribal people.

Gen. Gowon's 1966 message to the Northerners was a classic example of how pervasive tribalism is in Nigeria. In that message Gowon stated: "God in his power, has entrusted the responsibility of this great country of ours, Nigeria to the hands of another Northerner" (Kirk–Green 1974,62). Gowon must have been referring to the first defunct Republic's Prime Ministership of Sir Abubakar Tafawa Belewa, a Northerner. Since 1960, Nigeria has tended to be deficient in moral leadership or vision in matters of multiethnicity and socio–political underdevelopment. Most Nigerians have endeared tribal cohorts instead, while the nation as a whole continues to suffer socially, economically and politically.

But with the expanding population and the socio–political polarity, Nigeria is apt to face the reality of an impending national catastrophe from the vicious circle of poverty of the masses on one hand and elitism of the wealthy few on the other. The expectation is that with the continuous tribal squabbles, Nigeria could soon be faced, even overtaken by general hopelessness and mass starvation. African countries are already depending on foreign handouts to survive. The Washington Post's article has it that "the famines that resulted from wars in Nigeria Biafra region, Ethiopia, Sudan, Somalia and Rwanda are case in point" (Parmele 1994, A23). As Khit–Pen concept suggested, it is only when the cause of a problem is identified that one can find its solution. Nigeria needs a bigger dose of national consciousness to overcome its problems of today and tomorrow.

The existence of tribes and tribalism as part of African daily life was recognized by both Kwame Nkrumah and Patrice Lumumba. In advocating that the concept of tribes be separated from tribalism, they saw African underdevelopment as causing its tribalism. This position which we also endorse seems to imply that with an even development in society, tribal conflict and hatred can be eliminated. According to most social scientists, the consequences of downward mobility are similar [and] closely linked to that of underdevelopment in society. Merrill (1969, 234) stated that "persons who lack access to the means of gaining their life goals are marked by a psychological condition known as anomie." Anomie is defined sociologically as a condition marked with lack of standard norms and values caused by hopelessness and despair.

In general, when people are unhappy because of their low socio-economic statuses they tend to blame others who may or may not be responsible for their life condition. Lack of economic access has been known to encourage adversary group formation to fight the perceived oppressor, usually people from tribes other than their own. Without eradicating tribalism and poverty of the masses from Nigeria, its chances of ever achieving unity and democracy are slim. One outstanding evil of tribalism is the tricks it plays in the human subconscious and preventing one tribesperson from trusting the other wholeheartedly. Bishop G.G. Ganaka of Jos spoke about social conditions in Nigeria and identified this "lack of genuine love for others as another threat to the nation's continuous unity." (Jacob, 1994, 11).

Beginning in the 1940's, suggestions to solve the problem of tribalism in Nigeria was presented by the Eastern, Western and Northern leaders but usually in a negative fashion. Nothing received proper attention and hearing. The heinous problem of most Nigerians pretending to be nationalistic and still retaining tribal identities and values has always overshadowed their will to uphold issues intended for the common good. The issue of tribalism in Nigeria must be openly addressed.

Since independence, Nigerians, mostly military leaders have paid lip service to the issues of tribalism and have embraced instead a de facto segregation between different tribal groups. This is a defeatist attitude of divide and rule left behind at the end of the colonial rule. The tribal conglomeration which occurred in the colonial days has now produced Nigerian concubinage which, rather than live with the status quo of misery, hate and mistrust, an alternative lifestyle of divorce can be recommended. This view regained momentum in 1994 and may still be brewing. But those who hold the view that a break up in Nigeria will bring peace are also mistaken. The fact of the matter is that there is no region or state in Nigeria that is immune to ethnic plurality. In this wise, a united Nigeria is a more favorable option to provide Nigeria the benefits of its longterm goals.

Historically, the argument from inside and outside Nigeria has been heard that each of the three former regions, for example, can and should separately provide a somewhat ethnic homogeneity capable of minimizing ethnic strife. This view which is born out of the "Biafran mentality" is not only deceptive, full of social and political flaws, but also counterproductive to the overall need for Nigerians to develop a workable Nigerian type democracy and unity, and benefit from its past socio-political mistakes. Surely, those who are familiar with Nigeria would agree that ideological divisions are not limited to North, East and West, although such misguided delimitations had existed in the past. As debatable as this may be, based on historical events and political statements already discussed, there are the Middle Belt of Middle Northern people whose sociopolitical aspirations tend to be at variance with the rest of the Far Northerners. Other ideological in-groups can also be identified in the West and East as well.

In general, most social and political scientists have identified the following ideological groups in Nigeria : The Far Northerners, the Middle Northerners, the Westerners, the Central Easterners and the Southeasterners. The differences in political ideologies among these groups can be said to be nothing else but a disguise to perpetuate tribal politics and domination, inflamed by a system of self-serving historical data which have no bearing on today's socio-economic reality of the entire nation. Generally, by bringing up such historical cliché as language, religion or tribal origin, a tribal politician stands a chance of benefiting from these cheap shots to divide and rule. Language-wise, the West and the North seem to be more homogenous in their languages than the East. In the East, there are the Efiks, Ogojas, Ogonis, Ijaws, Ibos, and Ibibios devoid of an intergroup language. On the contrary, Hausa and Yoruba languages are widely spoken and understood in the North and West respectively.

The impact of language and religion in Nigeria's tribal relations has already been discussed for cross reference. At this point there is one question that needs to be asked. With all the anti-unity factors affecting Nigeria, why does Nigeria continue to exist as a nation? According to our assessment based on years of Nigerian political instability and other prevailing circumstances, the reason for its continuous existence seems to rest on the source of its income, the oil money; and the economic survivability of some of its parts. So, Nigeria's regions and states have clung together for years under the guise of ONE NIGERIA. Contrary to expectation, such economic interdependency has produced tribal arrogance instead of forging ethnic consensus, tribal militerism instead of tribal homogenity.

The conclusion is that the sociopolitical instability in Nigeria is not caused by ethnic diversity per se. This point was also brought home when we discussed global situations relative to ethnic diversity. Rather, Nigeria's instability is caused by the ingredient of its patrimonial tribalism.

NIGERIA: IDEOLOGICAL AFFILIATION
BY STATES AND REGIONS

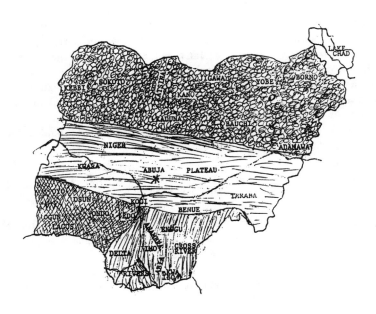

KEY

     Far Northern states

     Middle Belt states

     Western states

     East and Southern states

To benefit form "tribal nationalism" (Lumumba, 1978, 104) or tribal federalism, Nigerians must let go their clutches on tribalism and tribal rulership. Tribal nationalism cannot be achieved without the willingness (free will), determination and incentive of the tribes to coexist, to survive as a people, still retaining their tribal identities. This is one of the attributes which so adequately qualifies the United States of America as one nation in diversity. With this comparison, there should not be any difference [we think] in the patriotic pursuit between an Irish–American, German–American or African–American etc. in the United States and Ibibio–Nigerian, Tiv–Nigerian, Ibo–Nigerian etc in Nigeria respectively. In practical terms, this concept implies that all citizens of Nigeria be Nigerians first, tribesmen second.

To achieve the much needed unity, Nigeria must pursue the following broad initiatives:

1. Establish an agency for tribal studies ––to study, monitor and educate the public on tribal coexistence.

2. Establish and enforce the Human Bill of Rights, and make discrimination based on tribe, religion, and language a federal crime.

3. Establish sensitivity programs on ethnic diversity at all levels of education.

4. Discourage all tribal based political parties with regards to membership, funding and intent. Maintain a two–party system.

5. Have a national unity day (NUD) as a public holiday and a day of reflection.

6. Educate many Nigerians in law, preferably in American Constitutional law.

7. "Encourage inter–ethnic marriages" (Dr. Ukoh, 1994) even though we believe that marriage is personal and should not be forced or coerced but allowed to take its natural course of love between two people.

ISSUES OF CORRUPTION AND GREED

Corruption in public life takes different forms. It includes bribery or gift offering to curry favor, taking of public funds or properties for private use (embezzlement), unfair practices in public or private life, dishonesty and moral deterioration in society, to name a few. Greed, on the other hand, is defined as the excessive, insatiable and compulsive desire for wealth or gain. According to a dictionary definition, a compulsive behavior is an irresistible impulse to perform an irrational act. Any such behavior which cannot be terminated at will can be considered as psychosocially abnormal. Because corruption is akin to greed, it implies by definition that once a society or an individual starts along the path of corruption, stopping becomes increasing difficult or impossible unless it is followed by stringent legislations. According to the First Book of Samuel of the Holy Bible when judges were rulers, the sons of King Samuel who were made "judges over Israel...took bribes and perverted judgement" and consequently lost the throne of their father as punishment (1 S. 8:1–3).

Even though corruption in Nigerian national life did not become a household word until after Independence, its presence dates back to precolonial times when it was culturally acceptable for (Oba, Eze, Obong, Emir) the Chief to receive gifts such as cocks, goats, yams even cola nuts from his subjects in return for his blessings. In the Biblical account of the New Testament, there was nothing improper for the king's subjects to do the same. It is recorded that after Jesus was born in Bethlehem, "three wise men" presented unto him gifts: "gold, frankincense and myrrh" (Matthew 2:1). In both of these examples, gift offering was regarded as a gesture of goodwill and homage. In colonial Nigeria, however, the practice of gift offering (The Snapps Controversy) had a different meaning and implication, most especially under the Indirect Rule system.

The concept of control was always in the mind of the colonialists when they presented "hot drinks" to the native authorities. Native authorities had to be controlled to enable them to control their subjects in turn. So, it was all natural that the colonialists adopt a social system which was already an acceptable tradition within their so-called modernization framework. One point of importance must be emphasized. During the precolonial and colonial Nigeria, there was little or no separation between public and private ownership of wealth. In the precolonial era, the chief could dispense his wealth without accountability while in the colonial era, the colonialists under the grand scheme could dispense gifts or favors to the native elites so long as their ultimate objective of the indirect rule was achieved. This practice has led many to believe that corruption like tribalism as we know it today is a vestige of colonialism.

In post–colonial Nigeria, the perception of public and private wealth has remained pretty much undefined and undifferentiated. Consequently, most Nigerian leaders have continued to see themselves as chiefs and colonialists, not as public servants. In Nigeria today, there is a role conflict between the traditional norms on one hand and the modus operandi of the modern society on the other ––between public and private roles. Samuel P. Huntington associated corruption with modernization which has created new sources of wealth and power.

In Nigeria, for instance, the narcosis of the oil money and being in control of the most populous nation in Black Africa can be considered as the motivating factors of most Nigerian public officials. Huntington (1968,59) defined corruption as a "behavior of public officials which deviates from accepted norms in order to serve private ends," adding that:

> Corruption requires some recognition of the difference between public role and private interest. If the culture of a society does not distinguish between Lang's role as a private person and the Lang's role as a king, it is impossible to accuse the king of corruption in the use of public monies (p. 60).

The above statement describes adequately Nigeria's, in deed Africa's dilemma. The case in Zaire is another good example. In spite of Zaire's grim economic condition and the number of deaths reported due to malnutrition, Mobutu SeSe Seko who has been living comfortably in his palace has refused to give up power. Why? The reason is that like many leaders of other African countries, 'Mobutu thinks Zaire is his home. The bank is his pocket. All the women here are his wives' (Richburg 1993, A.16).

In order to erase role conflict in public service in African societies, there must be an updated ethical standard and criteria to define what an acceptable moral behavior of public officials ought to be. In Nigeria, however, adhering to a moral code in public life has proved unsuccessful for many decades for lack of effective control mechanisms. As a result each leader has managed to leave his public service two hundred–fold richer. With their loot and the help of some international agencies, organizations, even countries, most of these leaders have been able to live better lives than what they left behind, with whatever wealth they were able to extract from Nigeria. It is not surprising after Gen. Gowon was dethroned, he was able to take up his British residency while getting himself educated. Gen. Gowon might have set a trend in Nigeria's public life which has been difficult to break.

Corruption in Nigeria is reported by many as an epidemic. This is not limited to the military regimes. The concern is in their hypocrisy of "throwing the first stone," starting with the collapse of the Second Republic. Howard (1986, 137) stated that, "yet despite the predicted new stability of Nigeria polity, a military coup occurred on December 31, 1983. . . as is usual in Commonwealth Africa, the military cited corruption as a major precipitating cause." The one issue which we have agreed wholeheartedly with the Nigerian military is that there is corruption in Nigeria. But the big question has always been centering on who could bail the cat. The expectation was that with the military in charge, corruption in Nigeria would decrease, not increase. Contrary to this expectation, Buhari's promise to rid Nigeria of corruption failed miserably to achieve its goal. Through his draconian decrees he promised to punish those who dealt with counterfeit currency, sabotaged oil pipelines or power cables, dealt illegally on petroleum products or trafficked in cocaine.

Unfortunately his preventive detention Act: Decree No. 2 made matters worse. Under this decree, many Nigerians who criticized Buhari's regime for whatever reason, were detained. Prominent among his detainees was Dr. Tai Solarin – a newspaper columnist and educator whose detention lasted for more than one year. Buhari's military tribunal consisting of one civilian judge and three hand picked military members also left much to be desired. Both Decree No. 2 (Preventive Detention Act) and Decree No. 4 (Protection Against False Accusation Act) in spite of their nationalistic appearance, more than anything else seemed to protect Buhari's regime itself from charges of corruption. By the time Buhari was dethroned, a culture of corruption had already been cemented, inescapable by subsequent regimes. The concept of bloodless coups as a means of changing power was indicative of how much corruption in Nigeria had been syndicated and institutionalized. There tended to be in existence a syndrome of "You chop now and I chop later" normally among public officials and also among private citizens in all works of life.

In a Washington Post article entitled: *Nigerian Dictator Fires Three Labor Union Leaders*, the writer described Nigeria as "plagued by a string of oppressive, incompetent and corrupt military dictatorships" (Aigbogun 1994, A.13). Faul (1993, A.9) reported that:

> Corruption has been widespread in Nigeria for a long time but some political scientists say Gen. Babangida's administration has made it an instrument of state policies... For ordinary person, it is impossible to get services without paying a bit of 'a dash.' And many people can't get by without a little extras that make dey hand shine.

Like his predecessors, Gen. Abacha's declaration of war against indiscipline and corruption has made no progress. According to the Washington Post, Nigeria's "image problem" has induced the "Independent Lawyers' Association of Nigeria to form its own committee to fight fraud and drug trafficking which often go hand in hand here" (Shiner 1994, A.15). On April 4, 1994, Gen. Abacha himself acknowledged that 'drug trafficking has become a monumental national embarrassment and a cancerous malaise which is a great source of concern for [his] administration' (1994, a report from Embassy of Nigeria, Washington, DC). With that acknowledgement, it would be unusual for Nigerians not to expect something positive to happen in the drug trafficking and corruption fronts. But it appears that citizen's hopes in government as an effective intervention, to stop corrupt practices in the nation has dwindled beyond resurrection after so many years of recorded moral decay and lip service.

Power usurpation is another form of corruption in Nigeria which brings to mind the concept of illegitimacy of power and the manipulation of "ethnic sentiment to acquire political and economic resources" (Howard 1986,137). As we shall see later on, a legitimate power is the power of the people which is willingly given to a leader and can be withdrawn from him. Since Nigeria's Independence, many military coups to usurp power have taken place most of which have resulted either in a considerable loss of lives or uncontested imprisonment.

In Nigeria, power corruption is usually seen through the eyes of the beholder. In most cases, legitimacy of power depends on the outcome of a military coup or the ability of an individual to bribe himself to the position of power. From Gowon to Martala Muhamed, Dimka, Shagari, to Buhari, Babangida, Shonekan, Abiola and lastly to Abacha, the diagnosis of power and its illegitimacy has remained virtually that of getting it at all cost and desiring to be President for life.

In most third world countries like Nigeria, power legitimacy is not a description of the pathway to power but power itself. In 1993, the concept of legitimacy of power was raised when Gen. Babangida refused to give up power to the elected Moshood Abiola. According to the *Washington Post* report of August 7, 1993, Gen. Babangida's action was "criticized by his opponents as an attempt to transform the military ruler into a civilian leader" – an action which was successfully managed in Ghana under Jerry Rawlings. In 1994, Andy Shiner of the *Washington Post* described the Nigerian political power maneuver by apparently raising the question of the legitimacy of power.

In an article entitled: *Nigerian Opposition Leader Charged with Treason*, this author stated that "the government of Gen Sani Abacha who seized power from a military–appointed interim administration last fall, created a special court and chose its own attorney to prosecute Abiola" (Shiner 1994, A.13). Ironically, Mr. Abiola who was the elected President of Nigeria in the 1993 Presidential election was the one charged with treason for seemingly upholding democratic ideals, and opposing the military's action. Because of the apparent impropriety associated with the military in this regard, there was a general discontent in the country accompanied with labor strikes; notably the oil workers' union demanding the military to step down for Abiola.

In the past three decades, the manner in which power at the Federal level of government changed hands has raised serious disturbing questions about power corruption with regard to Nigeria vis a vis its political future. According to David Mark's statement to *Newswatch*, power corruption inside the military hierarchy was mentioned, affirming a planned militocracy in Nigeria. He stated that "the removal of Commodore Ukiwe by Gen. Abacha was calculated to put him in a position to usurp power when his friend Gen. Babangida leaves" (Mark, *Newswatch* 1994, 10).

For lack of space, the above discussion on corruption and greed in Nigeria is only an overview and not an item by item analysis of the problem. Nevertheless it reveals the urgency by which Nigeria must put its social and political life in order to regain its credibility geopolitically. This means that Nigeria must develop a system by which citizens are rewarded on merits in government and businesses so that they don't resort to bribery and corruption as a means of getting ahead. Greed can be controlled if Nigeria strives toward a classless society. To this end, initiatives which may not be limited to the ones listed below must be aggressively pursued either as government programs or as group effort toward establishing a workable society:

1. Teach ethics in government and in business at all levels of education.

2. Discourage bribery and corruption in society by developing worksite programs to be managed through special grants to the universities.

3. Improve employment and educational opportunities for all Nigerians.

4. Prevent embezzled monies from leaving the country.

5. Establish fairness in social, educational and economic systems.

6. Inculcate morality in society as part of religious worship involving Rabbi, Priest and Native doctors.

7. Discourage closing of educational institutions for political reasons.

8. Prevent politicians and public officials from leaving the country until their financial disclosures have been made.

9. Demand that citizens for public office declare their assets before and after public service.

10. Prosecute citizens for bribery and corruption.

11. Establish a Bureau Against Corruption (BAC) in all states to monitor and disclose bribery and corruption in public life.

12. Establish a system of Free Press and publication.

ISSUES OF THE ECONOMY
AND RESOURCE MANAGEMENT

Nigeria is the most populous nation in Black Africa. According to the 1990 World Population Data Sheet Nigeria has 118.8 million people. Nigeria enjoys an excellent tropical climate with little or no natural disaster problems like floods, hurricanes, tornadoes, landslides, or earthquakes. It has plenty of sunshine, rain and fertile lands for agriculture. Nigeria is blessed in many aspects of its ecological life – beautiful streams and lakes, seaports, streams and wildlife.

Nigeria cannot be considered as a poor country by virtue of its abundance of natural resources. Rather it is the tribal political conflict that has stifled its economic growth and marred its social equality. Under normal circumstances, if human skills and technology were matched adequately, a nation so endowed in natural resources should do well socially and economically. The reality is that Nigeria is still underdeveloped as determined by its vital social, economic and other demographic data, especially the declining per capita incomes.

Much of the data presented therein show Nigeria as a nation in economic decline. Its low economic, social and political status are somehow bewildering to many outside observers. Millions of Nigerians who have expected better results from Nigeria, instead are subjected to substandard lifestyles. This may be regarded as their worst let down by their leaders. Because of its abundance of wealth, Nigeria has been nicknamed the "Giant of Africa" and a land flowing with Black Gold. Among its outstanding natural resources are crude oil, and natural gas. According to reliable sources, other minerals such as tin, columbite, tantalite, wolfram, gold, lead–zinc, lignite, limestone, kaolin, thorium and Uranium have been suspected to exist in commercial quantities. Some of the minerals which Nigeria has already tapped in large commercial use are crude oil, coal, tin and Columbite.

Because Nigeria has rich lands and good weather conditions, agriculture has the potential of yielding large amounts of cash crops such as cocoa, palm produce, groundnut, rubber, hides and skin and cotton. Among the Nigerian staples are yams, rice, beans, cassava, millet, coffee, tobacco and assorted vegetables. Some of these staples and cash crops are also available at commercial quantities. Before Independence in 1960 and the discovery of crude oil, Nigeria depended totally on the production of palm oil, cocoa and groundnut to maintain

NIGERIA: APPROXIMATE LOCATION OF
VITAL NATURAL RESOURCES BY REGIONS

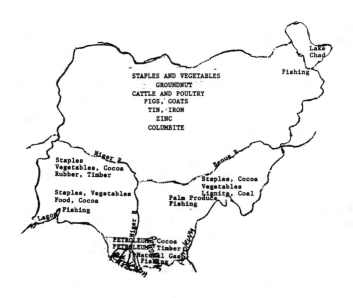

Source: From Patrick Smith, <u>Nigeria: Economy, Africa South of the Sahara</u>, 1994 London, England, Europa Publication P660–665; also see Federal Republic of Nigeria, National Youth Service Corps, (1973), p118–119. Service Corps (1973,119) reported that "at present, Nigeria is the third in the production of crude oil in Africa and eighth in the world."

its economy "accounting for more than one half of GDP and for more than three-quarters of export earnings" (Smith 1994, 661).

National income contribution by regions from agricultural products during the pre-colonial and colonial era had both social and psychological significance. Socially, each regional contributor was a national business partner with one another, each having a feeling of inter-regional belongingness. No region suffered the stigma of being a welfare recipient. Psychologically, regional contribution to the national economic upkeep generated inter-regional respect, pride and esteem for the region for their economic contributions. History has it that Nigerian farmers were motivated to change their lot in spite of a lack of support from the colonial masters, notably the fraudulent Colonial Development Act of 1929 in which Britain earmarked a meager 1 million pounds to "stimulate agricultural and industrial activity in the colonial territories...to relieve Britain of some of her own economic problems" (National Youth Service Corps 1973, 81).

Besides the production of cocoa for export in the West, and palm oil in the East, to the Nigerian economy, "the groundnut cultivation in northern Nigeria where the Hausa farmers planted the crop for export because of the higher monetary incentive they derived therefrom" (p. 82) also played a big part, all of which exemplified the entrepreneurial spirit of the pioneering Nigerians. The famous Groundnut Pyramid was once a source of pride of the northern people. Palm oil and cocoa production in the East and West respectively had the same impact on the Eastern and Western peoples, as well. Other products in the export category of the time were cotton and raw tin. But "the development of the petroleum industry in the late 1960s and 1970s radically transformed Nigeria from an agriculturally based economy to a major oil exporter" (Smith 1994, 660).

Consequently, the importance of agriculture for export and for domestic consumption has been declining, so has the pride of each region as an equal contributor to the national economic well being. To stress the degree of neglect on agriculture and complete dependency on oil alone to sustain the national economy, Smith pointed out that:

> ...in 1986, the petroleum industry accounted for around 18% of GDP, more than 95% of total export earnings and over 70% of all government revenues. In 1992 revenue from petroleum represented about 95% of the countries foreign exchange earnings (1994,662).

The dependency on petro–naria and the neglect of agriculture have had many other troubling effects on Nigeria. Many have come to regard the discovery of petroleum in Nigeria as a curse. Apart from the wasteful spending, corruption and national debt frequently associated with oil discovery, Nigeria has become complacent, less creative and less productive with regards to other sectors of the economy. Most importantly, the oil money which primarily comes from the Southeastern sections of the country has become a bone of contention. Nothing can be so true that oil has brought only poverty, degradation and now bitter feuding to the communities whose land is dug for the black gold that sustains Nigeria. The Ogoni controversey of the 1990s forms one example.

The main cause of Nigeria's political instability, underdevelopment, tribal oppression and numerous military coup d'etat is therefore the petro–naira which "are shared in decreasing proportions between federal, state and local governments..." (Smith 1994, 663). In our opinion, it is this revenue sharing formula from oil which has angered the oil producing states but compelled the ruling class [tribe] who is also the sole beneficiary from it to hang on to power at the center. It is noteworthy that in Nigeria crude oil has remained the property of the federal government rather than that of the oil–producing states. Like Lugard's Dual mandate in which the resource of Nigeria was spent elsewhere, other than in Nigeria, the utilization of the petro–naira, namely the revenue sharing, is controversial.

Opponents of the current revenue sharing system from oil would prefer that petro–naira be treated as revenues from agriculture products such as cocoa, palm produce and groundnut before the discovery of oil in Nigeria. Of course adhering to this suggestion may be farfetched as most Nigerians have come to embrace oil as an opportunity to get rich easily. They have forgotten how to till the soil and get their hands dirty. For them, shedding of blood and destablizing Nigeria are all worthwhile propositions to control the proceeds from oil.

Today, Nigeria having a per capita income of less than $300 makes it one of the world's poorest nations in spite of its oil wealth. The continuous "digging" of the estimated 1.98M b/d (1990) of crude petroleum for export amidst the decreasing living standards, social strife, and the decay of social amenities such as electricity, roads, running water, schools, hospitals, etc. have brought a worldwide disbelief. There has been a perpetual improper accounting system to show income and expenditure from petro–sale.

NIGERIA: PER CAPITA INCOME
IN U.S. DOLLARS 1984–1990

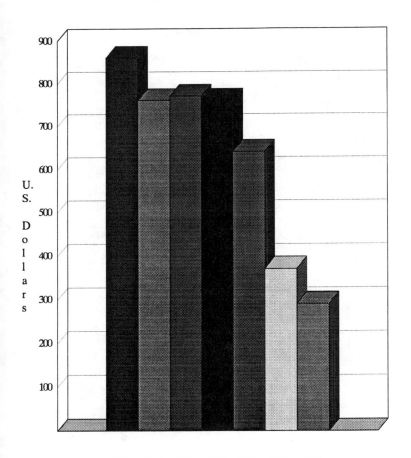

	1984	1985	1986	1987	1988	1989	1990
US$ in thousands:	860	760	770	760	640	370	290

Source: World Population Data Sheet, Population Reference Bureau, Inc., Washington, DC

We used to work with our hands...
then we went to school and. . .
                    discovered oil...

A typical example is the recent 1994 Central Bank of Nigeria (CBN) report of financial mismanagement already discussed. This economic waste and mismanagement of petro–naira has also remained a source of frustration to an average Nigerian who knows how well off he would have been under normal circumstances. In a recent Wall Street Journal article entitled: *Shell's Nigeria Fields Produce Few Benefits for Regions Villagers: Despite Huge Oil Revenue Firm and Government Neglect The Impoverished*, Brooks (1994) described the specific case of an accident caused by "oil slick oozing from a rupture in the pipeline" (p. 1) and an Ogoni woman – Grace Zorbidom who was burnt in an oil pipeline fire and yet neither Shell nor the Nigerian Military Government did anything to help the injured woman. Brooks also stated that:

> Mrs. Zorbidom's accident is just one of many instances in which Shell's presence, coupled with decades of the Nigerian Military government's own neglect, has damaged a vulnerable local community. Now tension is so high that Shell has had to shut down its operations in the area. Moreover, protests, even peaceful ones by unarmed peasants, have been violently suppressed by the military which often intervenes at Shell's request (Brooks 1994,1).

Much of the recorded fiscal mismanagement in Nigeria was generally associated with Shagari's and Babangida's administrations. In addition to the reported corruption and greed, different governments at different times also failed to demonstrate effective leadership in natural resource management and fiscal policy by neglecting resource conservation, diversification and long term investments for future economic self sufficiency. In a country like the U.S., Connelly and Perlman (1975, 98) stated that:

> resource position consists not merely in the generally higher ratios of self sufficiency which happens currently to have been achieved, but also in the totally superior endowment of resource reserves which remain to be tapped if and when circumstances make it necessary.

Among the Organization of Petroleum countries (OPEC), Nigeria's socioeconomic performance is ranked the poorest by per capita income comparison, living standards, and overall fiscal management. Nigeria's poor economic state is not an accident but rather a consequence of three main factors:

1.   Dependency on petro–naira as the sole source of national income.
2.   Tribalism and tribal related insecurities.
3.   Revenue sharing from petro–naira.

In spite of the overall gloomy picture about Nigeria, it is believed that if much of the natural resources were tapped resourcefully along–side with oil production, Nigeria would do well economically and socially. But this prediction can only be fulfilled if Nigeria gives up its self defeating habits relating to factors of tribalism, power narcissism, corruption, greed and irrational tribal fear and insecurities, all of which are linked to power narcissism of the tribal fundamentalists.

The belief in tribal power can be replaced with individual power, to empower individuals not the tribe, to be all they can be in society. There is a close similarity between the current Nigeria's tribal power system and the U.S. 19th century spoil system defined as ". . .the system or practice of making public offices the rewards of partisan services" (*Standard College Dictionary* 1963,1294). Schott (1974) cited some of the problems that faced the American bureaucracy of that century, drawing attention to the incompatibility of democracy and the spoils system. To defeat the spoils system in the U.S., this author explained that it was the "democratic spirit" combined with "ethos of individualism – a belief in the self–sufficiency and the self– reliance of the individual," adding that "the ideals of democracy and individualism served to reinforce what was to become a dominant theme of the nineteenth century American life – the doctrine of Laissez Faire" (Schott 1974,7).

Over the years, struggle for political power by tribe has been destructive to African nations. In an article entitled: *Africa 1994: Ecstasy and Agony*, the problem of African ethnic politics with specific emphasis to Rwanda formed the central theme. Here it was made clear that "it takes an extraordinary level of political leadership and political awareness of the population to overcome these destructive strategies" (Africa Demos, 1994,1). Similarly in Nigeria, those who hold power and would like to hang onto it seem to do so to control the petro–naira and to perpetuate tribal dominance. One report has stated that in general, Nigeria's rulers, both military and civilian have always been Northerners, and a few who are not of Northern origin usually inherit a government of which federal cabinet positions are Northern dominated. Anyanwu (1993) in an article entitled: *What Injustice Does*

NIGERIA AND OPEC:
PER CAPITA INCOME AND POPULATION

Country	Population In Millions (1990)	US$ Per Capita Income (1990)
Nigeria	118.8	290
Algeria	25.6	2,450
Venezuela	19.6	3,170
Libya	4.2	5,410
Saudi Arabia	15.0	6,170
Iraq	18.8	--
Iran	55.6	--
Kuwait	2.1	13,680
Indonesia	189.4	430
Gabon	1.2	2,970
Qatar	0.5	11,610
Ecuador	10.7	1,080
United Arab Emirates	1.6	15,720

Source: World Population Data Sheet, Population
Reference Bureau, Inc., Washington, D.C.

to A Man discussed Nigeria's institutional injustice," and called for an end to it. He stated that "since the war ended, the East was left in the backwaters of neglect and deprivation. However, growing awareness promises a new era of self assertiveness of the people" (p. 12). To invalidate an economic neglect in the East due to its power deficiency, Anyanwu stated that, "the Gowon/Murtala/Obasanjo regimes committed its proceeds to the development of infrastructure in the West and the North especially Lagos, Kaduna and Kano" (p. 16). He stated that while an estimated 93% of the federal revenue came from East, the so called adjunct region, only 10% of the revenues was earmarked for its development.

In recent years, following the annulment of the election which Mr. Mushood Abiola supposedly won, the Yoruba speaking South Westerners have become belatedly anxious to see Northern political dominance and the uneven distribution of revenue end. As would be expected this movement resulted in a tumultuous action and counteraction basically between West and North that ended in Abiola's detention. According to human right sources, close to 100 people were killed following the detention. Essentially, the intertribal grudges which stifles Nigeria's growth and development is rooted in petro–naira; who controls it and who does not.

Because the petro–Naira and the Central Bank of Nigeria (CBN) have been the only symbols of the fragile federation since 1962, the many years of intertribal fighting, military takeover, even the civil war have all represented the struggle for power control instigated by greed and corruption, short and simple. Hence, being a president or commander in chief of the armed forces or a Cabinet member in Nigeria has become in many ways not only an attractive and lucrative business but also a gate opener for instant wealth by the individuals concerned. The understanding is that there is "plenty of money to chop" by the ruling tribe, despite political instability, crippled national economy, uneven development and underdevelopment in some parts of the society.

One of these petro–naira motivated "get rich quick" episodes occurred during Shagari's regime when the nation was still in its infancy. Angered by the amount of money being shipped out of Nigeria by corrupt politicians, Gen. Buhari was determined to act partly to recover the loot or bring those concerned to justice. McCaskie (1994, 660) cited as an example the 1984 "attempted kidnapping in London of Umaru Dikko, a political exile and former minister in the Shagari

NIGERIA: POWER DISTRIBUTION AT THE
FEDERAL LEVEL OF GOVERNMENT BY FOUR MAIN
REGIONS 1960 – 1993

Federal Cabinets, Leadership and Composition	Mid-west	West	North	East
Dr. Azikiwe – Governor General 1960 (East) Sir Belewa – Prime Minister 1965 (North)	8	14	22	15
Supreme Military Council – Ironsi 1966 (East)	0	2	3	1
Federal Executive Council – Gowon 1966 (North)	2	3	2	0
Supreme Military Council – Murtala 1975 (North)	1	7	13	1
Supreme Military Council – Obasanjo 1976 (West)	2	7	8	1
Ministers & Junior Min. – Shagari 1979 (North)	2	7	23	8
Supreme Military Council – Buhari 1984 (North)	3	2	11	2
Armed Forces Ruling Coun. – Babangida 1985 (North)	3	8	15	4
Armed Forces Ruling Coun. – Babangida 1989 (North)	2	2	6	1
Armed Forces Ruling Coun. – Babangida 1992 (North)	2	5	10	1
Nat. Defense & Sec. Coun. – Babangida 1993 (North)	1	5	6	0
Transitional Council – Babangida 1993 (North)	3	5	16	5
Interim Nat. Gov't – Shonekan/Babangida 1993 (North)	3	7	15	7
Totals in 33 years	32	74	150	46

Source: Adapted from Chris Anyanwu, 1993 What Injustice Does To A Man, *The Sunday Magazine*, Oct. 3, pp 19–20

administration who was being sought for trail in Nigeria on charges of corruption." Since late 1970s, to date, Petro–Naira grabbing has been non–stop. Around mid September of 1994, a panel report investigating the Central Bank of Nigeria on the order of Gen. Abacha concluded that between 1988 and June 1994, Nigeria military rulers squandered $12 billion.

Political aspiration in Nigeria, be it the presidency or any high office of the land should not be motivated by personal ambition of subjugating others or by the fact that there is "plenty of money to chop" at the top. Rather, there ought to be that need to respond to a higher calling to serve the country with fairness, honor, integrity, dignity and remuneration. Serving one's country properly is to be accountable to the people and to ensure that by one's decisions and actions future generations can do better socially and economically, not worse. The incentive to hold a public sector job should be the desire to serve one's country while the incentive for the private sector job should be to increase the profit margin – to be rich. When these two ideas are effectively combined and accepted, they serve to uphold the principle of democracy and free enterprise system.

To have political stability, social and economic growth in Nigeria, there must be a rule of thumb to follow in addition to a market driven economy where all citizens earn incomes through work which is supported by effective government policies. A market economy is not complete unless it is supplemented by "democratization of the political process by which the public will of the state is becoming established" (Myrdal 1960, 37).

For the most part, Nigeria has come to depend solely on the petro–naira to buy goods and services in lieu of productive work – a sort of corrupted welfare system where government subsidies from oil go to support indolences. Above all, the dependency on petro–naira has an adverse psychological effect of creating a false sense of economic security in a country and the capacity to discourage sectoral natural resource development. On the human capital, it has a debilitating effect on competitiveness, ingenuity and innovativeness.

To bring about political stability, Nigeria needs a redirection in its current political policies as well as in the treatment of public finance. It must encourage and revitalize sectoral agricultural and industrial economies, establish regional trade based on the principle of comparative cost advantage, restore pride of work to all Nigerians, allow for free enterprise system of private ownership, establish a system for honest pay for honest work, and establish a tax and tariff systems to financially support the states and the federal government. Above all the central government must be detracted from its sole financial source. Its familiar politico–economic culture must be changed. This means that current resource and revenue sharing policies must be revised, giving less financial power to the central government. A financially weakened central government, in our opinion, is likely to create a unified Nigeria, politically. The following longitudinal resource and revenue revision plan is proposed to enhance the above broad goals:

1.   That crude oil remains the property of the central government for 5 years beginning from year 1995 in which the revenue from petroleum is shared equally among states with a prepaid 5% flat tax to the federal government.

2.   That crude oil remains the property of the central government for 5 years beginning from year 2000 in which oil producing states are allowed 10% additional money with 5% prepaid flat taxes to the Federal government.

3.   That crude oil remains the property of the oil producing states [private ownership] beginning from year 2005 in which income taxes of 5% and tariff are paid to the Central government by the states.

4.   That Federal revenues be based on tariffs and a 5% flat income tax charged to individuals and states, etc.

5.   That private entrepreneurship of each state be encouraged to spearhead regional investment, productive work, competition, trade and education.

6.   That Central Bank of Nigeria (CBN) be put under the trusteeship of the National People Ruling Committee (NPRC) with the power of the chairman to appoint its governor from state nominations.

ISSUES OF DEMOCRACY

At the end of the Colonial Rule in 1960, Nigeria faced the dilemma of creating a workable society based on democratic ideals. This problem

**NIGERIA: SUGGESTED FEDERAL REVENUE IN STATE
INCOME TAXES IN MILLIONS OF NAIRA
PER FISCAL YEAR**

Example:

States	Income by States	Percent	Federal Revenue
A	₦100	5	₦5.00
B	₦120	5	₦6.00
C	₦300	5	₦15.00
D	₦450	5	₦22.10
E	₦600	5	₦30.00
F	₦0	5	₦0
GNP	₦1570	5	₦78.1

is as acutely felt today as it was the very day the colonialists parked their baggage. Since their departure, there has been a mismatch between the imported systems of governance and the African culture they were purported to serve. But most political scientists are being less sympathetic with the current political malaise in Africa in general and in Nigeria in particular. While most scientists have accepted the linkage between colonialism and African decay, colonialism and enslavement, the sympathy hitherto enjoyed by Africa based on years of colonialism is declining. Most people tend to believe that African countries have had ample time and resources to adjust and to create their own forms of democratic governments, but instead their leaders have lacked the ambition and foresight in this direction. Nigeria for that matter, with its abundance of resources, has no excuse for its socio–economic malaise. Makanju (1994, 1) discussed Nigeria's numerous problems and declared that "a quick return to democratic governance has been identified. . .as a crucial requirement for the restoration of the nation's economic glory."

The struggle for democracy and self–government in Africa as a whole has been unique, stretching over a few decades. In retrospect, 1940s can be remembered globally as the decade of insurgency of political self determination. In Africa this struggle has been continuous into the 1990s with no end in sight. In 1945 after WWII, the UN passed its Charter calling for individual basic human rights and fundamental freedom. The UN Charter was to lay the groundwork for self governance, and enfranchisement of the oppressed and the colonized. Hence, for 50 years (1940s–1990s), many African nations came face to face with the problem of decolonization, voting rights and political participation. It was through this process that African countries obtained their independence, primarily in the 1960s which dangerously exposed them to the ramifications of self–rule.

Then came the globalization of democracy. In 1980s, the concept of democracy received more impetus and was perceived globally as the only vehicle through which the individual basic human rights, fundamental freedom and market economy can be achieved in full. It was not just sufficient for nations to be independent without complying with the U.N. Charter. In other words, the concept of independence would only be regarded as complete when democratic ideals were adhered to. Consequently, many dictatorial regimes were pressured much more than before to change. These pressure groups included national freedom fighters, international organizations and the world's leading democracies.

In the same period, Eastern Europe, the Soviet Union, China, North Korea became the first group of countries to face relentless ideological assault from the West. The leadership roles of Ronald Reagan of the United States and Margaret Thatcher of Great Britain were significant, leading to the former Soviet Union being declared the "evil empire." Internal freedom fighters used both violent and nonviolent demonstrations towards those regimes that resisted political reform. Leading democracies of the 1980s that made the most contributions toward global democratization included the United States, Great Britain, West Germany and France working with other countries through the UN General Assembly, the Security Council, and the UNEF. Such pressures and contributions were apparent and had brought partial results in the former Soviet Union, South Africa, Haiti and in parts of South America. They also helped in exposing and preventing human rights abuses in China and North Korea. In most of these cases, force was necessary to obtain compliance from dictatorial regimes.

Most African dictatorships of the 1980s and 1990s, like Nigeria, have received international condemnation in the form of political pressure and economic sanctions to no avail. African dictatorships are oftentimes entrenched and can easily escape the scrutiny of international public opinion. After African decolonialization and recently the cold war, most African countries are not usually considered as economically or militarily strategic to the West i.e. not posing a threat to their national security. Without the presence of a national security threat to donor nations, like the United States, France, Great Britain and West Germany, mobilizing their public opinion to support an African initiative to stop human rights abuses is usually an uphill battle. Even Nigeria with its oil wealth has failed to qualify as a candidate for strong global intervention. Rather it is the oil benefit to the world that has perpetuated the dictatorial rule in that part of the world.

Some of the military interventions or economic sanctions to African dictatorial regimes are mostly for humanitarian efforts, usually assigned to the U.N. which we have described as a toothless bulldog. Most African dictators having understood this international political game have exploited it to their fullest advantage. Most African dictators have been known to be heartless and selfish to their people. Buckley (1995, A28) stated that "Sunday marks Nigeria's 35th anniversary of independence from Britain, but many Nigerians believe they are still shackled." This assessment may be based on Nigeria's deteriorating political and economic conditions, recurrent human right abuses and lack of democracy. The outcome of the U.S. led military invasion of Somalia in 1993 to stop civil war atrocities of Mohamed Farah Aideed was one lesson to be learned about the craftiness of most African dictatorships.

In post colonial Africa, the direct correlation between its dictatorships and socio–economic deterioration of the continent is clear. There are reported cases of shortages of food and medical supplies causing deterioration in general human conditions. African dictatorial power unlike democratic power is basically the power of the powerholder to control others while enriching himself and his family. Under such dictatorial rule, detentions, false imprisonment and decision making are usually done by one person or a handful of power usurpers operating under emergency laws and/or military decrees. African dictators have done much damage to Africa and its people, and there is an immediate need for African democratization. Nigeria, for example, is overdue for democracy given its 35 years of independence from Britain in 1960.

Historically, many countries have embraced democracy after the disappearance of their despots. Morse (1970) listed some of the past well known despots whose nations have since become democratic when he wrote:

> in modern times, men who have assumed power over the state have been called dictators, notable among these have been Porfinio Diaz of Mexico, Miguel Primo de Rivera and Francisco Franco of Spain, Kemal Ataturk of Turkey, Jose Pilsudski of Poland, Antonio de Oliveira Salazar of Portugal, Benito Mussolini of Italy, Adolf Hitler of Germany and Joseph Stalin of the Soviet Union (p. 2740).

In recent years, while dictatorial rule seems to be decreasing elsewhere in the world, it is increasing in most parts of Africa in spite of its unpopularity. Nigeria for example has been virtually ruled dictatorially since the Civil War of 1967. Faul (1993, A1) stated that: "Nigeria has been under military rule for 23 of its 33 years of independence." Faul (1993), on the possibility of democracy in Nigeria, stated that "Nigeria's mercurial military ruler has taken this nation deeper into a dizzying maze filled with dead ends and sharp turns, with democracy waiting at the other end, wherever that is" (p. A11). Fritz (1993) reported on the number of deaths as Nigerian rioters clashed with the local police in their demand to "end military dictatorship" (p. A23).

With the developing trend of dictatorship in Africa, be it in Ghana or in Nigeria, there is need to investigate reasons behind African dictatorship. In an article entitled: *Democracy in Africa: One Step Forward, One Back,* Shiner (1994, A27) pointed out 'how South Africa shamed Nigeria' and commented on the inconsistencies in actual practice of democracy in Nigeria and in other parts of Africa. The point is that Nigeria – the Giant of Africa was expected to lead the way in democratic reform in Africa, not South Africa. Accordingly, south African apartheid was dismantled in 1992, paving the way for its democracy. As was pointed out earlier, many questions are being asked about the failure of democracy in most African nations like Nigeria. Improper management of tribal or ethnic, religious and linguistic diversity inter alia have already been cited with regularity as causing and protecting African dictatorship instead of promoting its democracy.

In an article entitled: *Will Africa Democracy Work,* Richburg (1992) found out that African rulers themselves have the tendency to follow "the colonial regimes they replace" (p. C5) instead of trying to carry out the mandate of the people. Single–party or military regimes backed by civilian elite has been more favorable to African rulers because they believe that they can say 'stop it and the people would stop because they are afraid' (p. C5). Leaders like Danial Arap Moi of Kenya have maintained that the [African] people are not "ready for democracy." The fact of the matter is that most of these African leaders belonging to the old school have lacked the backbone to try new ways, to give up power once they get it. It is our belief that even if a politician believes he is giving his best in office but is rejected by the people, he should gracefully resign his office.

To the contrary, like the Colonialists, most African leaders, insisting on conducting the business of governoring the old fashioned way, never leave power voluntarily. Staying on in office should not be the decision of the leader–politician but that of the led. Hodgkin (1957, 170) stated that "the theoretical weapons with which African nationalists make their revolutions have been largely borrowed from the armories of the metropolitan countries. Much of the political thinking of contemporary African leaders are bound to be derivative." In a document entitled: *Africa: Dispelling the Myth,* written by the Washington Office on Africa for the Africa Peace Tour (WOA), it is stated that:

the colonial era left Africa with a legacy of authoritarian rule. Borders dissected ethnic groups. The new government took over states as defined by the Colonial powers and consolidating a national identity became a primary focus after independence. In many cases this was used as an excuse to consolidate power in the elite and to eliminate opposition. Today a new generation of Africans is demanding a 'second Independence' to create more responsive political system open to grassroots participation (WOA 1992,1).

The missing link in all of this is that most African dictators have failed to realize that even though the colonialists ruled Africa dictatorially, their home countries were governed democratically – from Renaissance to Reformation to Industrial Revolution. For example, Adam Smith (1723–90) was a Scottish national whose concept of the Invisible Hand in the *Wealth of Nations* had brought Britain individual human freedom, business freedom and prosperity. Plato, a Greek philosopher (427–347 B.C.) in the *Republic* defined the ingredient of the "ideal state" to include the presence of values and good life for the individual and for the State as a worthwhile goal for that individual or state to achieve. He also maintained that truth can only be formed through discussions, clash of ideas and personalities.

Plato's concept of the philosopher–king should not pose any controversy regarding his conviction on how a state should be ruled. Plato believed that the state should produce the best and the brightest people and that only the qualified and wise should rule. If Plato's statement meant rulership by a king or a selected few, as has been widely misinterpreted, his idea of an ideal state would have been contrary to the conviction of the Greeks who believed in "moral value of the law and the participation of citizens in the task of self government" (Hartfield, 1971, 153).

Socrates (470–399 B.C.) also a Greek basically believed that citizens are bound by conscience to obey the laws of the state. Aristotle (384–322 B.C.), another Greek philosopher believed that governments should be ruled by laws and not by men regardless of how wise and good men may be. He also believed that both the ruler and the ruled have moral obligations to equally obey the laws of the State. In spite of these philosophical and ideological developments which favored democracy in Europe, continental Africa instead was exposed to a tyrannic system, disguised to meet the economic means of its oppressor. Africa did not benefit from the Renaissance, Reformation or Industrial

Revolution and hence for centuries had no basis of relating to democratic ideals from which to establish African democracy.

If Reformation in Europe meant freedom of worship and political association, Africa was once again paid with a bad coin. Africa was not allowed the freedom to worship as it pleased, instead it was coerced into a faulty political lifestyle and religion of the colonizers. Besides improper orientation on ideals of democracy and capitalism which often go hand in hand, most African Countries including those ruled by the father of capitalism, Britain, were left to fend for themselves after obtaining their independence. Consequently, most African countries like Nigeria experimented different forms of political self–governance such as socialism, monarchism, civilian dictatorship, military dictatorship and democracy without any hope of a long term success.

African leaders had also become leery of capitalism because under colonial capitalism in Africa the colonialists became richer while the Africans became poorer. Somehow frustrated, most African leaders of the 1960s, like Julius Nyerere of Kenya had once considered socialism as a means by which underdeveloped countries of Africa could gain strength and combat capitalistic exploitation, oppression and maltreatment. He saw newly independent Africa as weak politically, economically and socially. Nyerere then believed that "socialism can be compatible with our aspirations: by adopting socialist policies it is possible for us to maintain an independence and develop towards human dignity for all our people" (p. 123).

Because of these sad experiences which have been ongoing, suggestions have surfaced every now and then urging Africa to revert to the traditional method "with a paramount Chief ruling over each state" (National Youth Service Corp., 1973,27). if stability in Africa is to be attained. The reason is that there are some Africans who have considered democracy as alien to Africa. We have found such considerations to be moot due to the social, political and economic changes since the pre–colonial era. In the face of all odds, Africa, indeed Nigeria needs to understand that today, Democracy is the right form of self governance. Besides being geopolitically acceptable, Democracy has been deemed to guarantee economic prosperity and political stability to depressed nations. Based on this observation, two basic questions have arisen. The first question is, what is democracy? The second one is, can Nigeria be democratically governed?

Democracy has been defined as a form of government in which political power resides in all the people and is exercised by them directly (pure democracy), or is given to elected representatives (representative democracy), with each citizen sharing equally in political privilege and duty, and with his right to do so protected by free elections and other guarantees. (Funk and Wagnall's Standard College Dictionary, 1963, 355)

The word democracy is derived from two Greek words: Demos meaning "the people" and *Kratein* meaning "to rule." In the early days and in accordance with democratic ideals, all citizens could speak or vote in a town meeting and no one could be denied the right to speak or vote. Public decisions were made based on the outcome of such an open and fair process. This process was called Direct Democracy and was widely used in self governance during the pre–christian era. It is worthy to mention that direct democracy could only succeed among small populations of people. But as the world's population increased a different method of political participation was adopted known as representative democracy.

The origin of democracy as is practiced today is found in the Renaissance which swept Western Europe in the 15th century resulting in intellectual and cultural movement. Because the Renaissance was limited to Western Europe, Italy, Britain, France, West Germany, Africa and Eastern Europe have been lagging behind in democratic idealism. But this should not be taken as an excuse to become inactive in the 20th century participation in the spirit of Renaissance and Reformation.

Renaissance was followed by Reformation and Secularism aiming at winning religious, political and social rights for every human being from the autocracy of the Roman Church and the Papacy. At that time also, the importance of the Stoic philosophy which amplified the teaching of Socrates and Plato, advocated the brotherhood of man and the natural equality of all human beings was heavily emphasized. The American democracy for example can be regarded as the product of the Western European Reformation movement when European dissidents left the shores of Europe for the "new world" to establish the first 13 colonies in America. To them, democratic idealism of freedom, voting and fundamental human rights were cherished as life itself. Today many Americans have come to regard Democracy as Life. Cohen (1994) related democracy to economic prosperity and stated that:

Democracy also means that people are empowered to make their decisions within a general context of the rule of law...gives people freedom to make their own decisions and to react to economic signals from the market place (p. 5).

Modern democracies are based on the same basic democratic principles as practiced in the pre-christian era. The concept of representation which is widely used today means that every one should have a voice in the manner in which he is governed. Its main features are individual freedom, equality before the law, universal suffrage and education. It also utilizes representatives who are voted into political offices to act as surrogates. They can be voted out if the mandate of the people is not carried out. Historically, these features can be traced to such documents as the American Declaration of Independence, emphasizing the right to life, liberty and the pursuit of happiness; the French Declaration of the right of men and citizens, meaning equality before the law and civil liberty.

Morse (1970, 2685) stated that "while the ideals of democracy have been widely professed, the practice and the fulfillment have lagged behind in varying degrees for countries." This last point brings us to the second question of importance which we raised earlier and that is, can Nigeria practice democracy? The answer is "yes" but there must be a conscious effort on its part towards meeting the necessary prerequisite for democracy. Citizens must be taught and they must believe that democracy is the overwhelming accepted form of government in today's geo-politics. The political culture based on a two-party system must be developed. Winter and Bellows (1981, 98) defined this culture as "a widely shared rules, values, norms, cognitions and ways of life of the members of a particular group."

There are two main types of political ideologies, Democracy and Socialism, with others falling in between. A political party ideology or belief must be carefully formulated and presented in the manner and language that every citizen must understand. A party ideology or belief, as derived from a political ideology, is a plan of action for a country, pointing out the national goal and how that goal is to be achieved in time and place. Most political scientists would agree that societies seem to perform well if the political culture is nationalistic. Generally, most countries operate under a single party, two-party and multi-party systems. In the past, Nigeria unsuccessfully experimented a multi-party democracy. Most of these parties were tribal parties in orientation.

Before 1989, the political parties, as listed in the following table, had made their marks in the Nigerian political system. On October 1989, the National Electoral Commission (NEC) was formed on the advice of the Armed Forces Ruling Council (AFRC) to start a political process for party organization. The goal was to return the military regime to the civilian government. Thirteen political associations were formed from which NEC presented only 6 to AFRC. These six political associations were later discarded by AFRC. They were replaced with "two new political parties, the Social Democratic Party (SDP) and the National Republic Convention (NRC)" (McCaskie 1994, 657).

When the two–party federalism was initiated by Gen. Babangida, it signalled hope for Nigeria's democracy and a dissipation of tribal politics. These national dreams remained alive until the unexplainable annulment of June 12, 1993 Presidential election by the military leadership. Before the annulment of that Presidential election and the two–party system, political institutions at local and state levels of government were up and running. It called to question the motive behind the military's action. According to Newswatch (1994), David Mark stated that [Babangida] "he certainly had the best opportunity to transform Nigeria and imprint his name in gold, but unfortunately he allowed his friends like Abacha to derail him and frustrate his laudable programmes" (p. 17).

The sooner Nigeria adopts a two–party federalism as the first step to democracy, the better its chances, not only in attaining political stability but also putting an end to the longstanding tribal hegemony. Nigeria's two party system can be regarded as the only political mechanism to force a multi–tribal alliance of all Nigerians into two main political camps such as SDP and NRC. It can enable them to elect national instead of tribal leaders at the federal levels of government. Undoubtedly, this arrangement is likely to threaten the stronghold of the de facto tribal power, oftentimes achieved either through a military dictatorship or a multi–party system of exploitation and manipulation of the underprivileged tribes into an illicit political party coalition. In general, most enduring democracies have worked well in a two–party system. Even though Winter and Bellows (1981) have pointed that "two–party systems are limited a few countries, principally the United States, Great Britain, New Zealand, Austria and West Germany" (p. 181) these numbers may be changing.

NIGERIA: EVOLUTION OF POLITICAL PARTIES
1960 – 1989

Party Acronym	Party Name	Party Leadership	Party Origin & Tribal Origin
UPN	Unity Party of Nigeria	Awolowo	Action Group (AG) Western (Yoruba)
UPGA	United People Grand Alliance	Azikiwe & Shagari	Coalition of NCNC & NPC North & East
PRP	People Redemption Party	Aminokano	Northern Element Progressive Union (Nepu) Northerner (Hausa–Fulani)
GNPP	Great Nigerian Peoples Party	----	----
NPN	National Party of Nigeria	Shagari	Northern Peoples Congress (NPC) Northerners (Hausa–Fulani)
NPP	Nigerian Peoples Party	Azikiwe	National Congress of Nigerian Citizens (NCNC) Easterners, Ibo, Ibibio, etc.
SDP	Social Democratic Party	----	National participation
NRC	National Republican Convention	----	National participation

NIGERIA: STATES, CAPITALS, POLITICAL PARTIES & LOCAL GOVERNMENT AREA

STATES	CAPITALS	PARTY	NUMBERS OF L.G.A. IN EACH STATE
Lagos	Ikeja	SDP/NRC	15
Enugu	Enugu	NRC/SDP	19
Kaduna	Kaduna	NRC	18
Kano	Kano	NRC	34
Ondo	Akure	SDP	26
Benue	Makurdi	SDP	18
Plateau	Jos	SDP	26
Akwa Ibom	Uyo	NRC	24
Edo	Benin	SDP	14
Bauchi	Bauchi	NRC	23
Oyo	Ibadan	SDP	25
Imo	Owerri	NRC	21
Rivers	Port–Harcourt	NRC	14
Katsina	Katsina	NRC	26
Ogun	Abeokuta	NRC	15
Adamawa	Yola	NRC	16
Borno	Maiduguri	SDP	21
Niger	Minna	NRC	19
Sokoto	Sokoto	NRC	33
Cross River	Calabar	NRC	14
Kwara	Ilorin	SDP	12
Abia	Umuahia	NRC	17
Delta	Asaba	SDP	19
Jigawa	Dutse	SDP	21
Kebbi	Birinin Kebbi	NRC	16
Kogi	Lokoja	NRC	16
Osun	Oshogbo	SDP	23
Taraba	Jalingo	SDP	16
Yobe	Damaturu	SDP	12
Anambra	Awka	SDP	16

ROTATIONAL VS. PARTICIPATORY PRESIDENCY

Nigeria's fundamental problem is its inability to forge a central government devoid of tribalism and irrational fear of tribal domination. In the past most federal elections had not only produced "hell" but also instability due to an overall inability of Nigeria to elect and retain a working President, let alone honor its constitution. In the quest for what works in Nigeria's political life, a rotational presidency on a zonal or state basis has been suggested by many policy makers, even at the 1994 constitutional conference at Abuja.

Proponents of rotational Presidency have long maintained that it would enhance power sharing and perhaps provide continuity in government. But, no workable rotational plan has been offered. All that is known thus far is that there would be 6 zones which the presidency must rotate, each for X number of years. Okoh (1994, 21) concluded his treatise by suggesting that:

> The two year rotational presidency among the states in Nigeria will bring political stability, peace, economic development and prosperity. The two year rotational presidency among the states in Nigeria would hasten the elimination of Neocolonialist stooges in Nigeria...

We observe a rotational presidency as providing no bright political future for Nigeria. The speculation is that rotational presidency is detrimental to a country where nationalism is weaker than tribalism. Its implementation is likely to produce a culture of corrupt and opportunistic ruling oligarchy. The fear is that power entrusted in any ethnic group will lead to an uneven development during its term in office. This problem has been cited earlier in the preceding pages. Additionally, in a rotational presidency, the familiar "struggle for political leadership in the Nigerian State among the three 'major' ethnic groups in a multiethnic Nigerian polity" (Okoh 1994,1) is likely to become a struggle or tribal war within the state or zone whose turn it would be to produce a president.

It is our hope that Nigeria would like to put the experience of the 1962 Western Crisis between the supporters of Awolowo and Akintola behind it by making every effort to nationalize its political system. We envision a stable Nigeria as depending on state nationalism. Any political and economic strength of the Central government should flow

NIGERIA: POLITICAL ZONES BY STATES

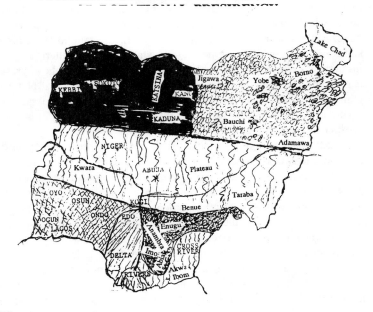

KEY

 Northeast Zone

 Northwest Zone

 Middle Belt Zone

 East Central Zone

 Western Zone

 Minority Southern Zone

from the states and the local communities where the people live, work and can elect their own political representatives to all levels of government. Fragmentation of Nigeria, other than states, into pockets of ideological camps should have ended with colonialism. Nigeria's policy makers should not forget that ethnic mistrust in Nigeria is endless – a point which has been emphasized repeatedly. Political polarity in Nigeria can not be viewed from a geographical standpoint of regions, states or zones. In each of the regions, states or zones, there are "small in–between ethnic groups" – the interkindred groups – whose presence can be and has been disruptive to a smooth political process. Nations so ethnically polarized as Nigeria but has the need to confederate, must seek courses of action to attain the goal of living together in peace and prosperity.

Last but not least, rotational presidency is exclusionary relative to a comprehensive democratic process of choosing national leaders. It does not afford all members of society equal opportunity in time and place to participate in an electoral process. Citizens from zones other than the one producing the president may not have the chance or motivation to exercise their national duty. Remember that in order for a democracy to work, citizens of adult suffrage must vote.

Based on the above analysis, it seems that Nigeria is heading toward another dead end plan with a rotational presidency. Nigeria does not need nor can it afford a presidential government as it currently exists in a country like the United States. Rather a central government which is multiethnic just as the country is, could be satisfactory to promote a lasting peace and stability for that tribal–torn country. Nigeria is a unique nation based on its tribal diversity. Consequently it needs a system of government which is fair, and can minimize the headache and the cost of trying to elect a "president."

Too much power can not be put into one person's hand without making him a dictator. The same can go with a tribe. In Nigeria, it is not unusual for political leaders to engage in a cooptative tribal nepotism for the purpose of power consolidation. As a consequence, there are some tribes in Nigeria which can be cited as being at the verge of engaging in tribal dictatorship based on population size, religion and control of the armed forces.

Past experience, if not common sense, dictates that something as controversial as electing one person as president of Nigeria should better be left alone. The 1992 Nigeria's presidential primaries is one example in which according to the *1992 Associated Press* report of the

Washington Post 'illegal use of wealth, intimidation and other forms of electoral fraud' (p. A36) dominated the entire electoral process in most states and forced its cancellation. Ayeni (1992) pointed out that in that election the "events revealed that the total number of votes purported to have been cast exceeded those on the registers of party members of the two parties" (p.1386).

The appropriate national political plan for Nigeria in our opinion is the participatory government managed by a 30–31 member Nigerian Peoples' Ruling Committee (NPRC) of state representatives or presidential delegates who will govern by consensus. Winter and Bellows (1981,514) have defined a participatory political system as a "type in which a significant number of citizens have legal means, usually through elections to influence or determine important political decisions." One important prerequisite in this plan is obvious. The plan should be carefully crafted and constitutionally cemented so that persons serving in government consist of only bright, resourceful, well–educated nationalists, capable of operating within a team spirit. Strong leadership is also important and should come from the majority party in NPRC. Any party (NRC or SDP) which forms a simple majority in the NPRC will provide the leader (Mr. Chairman) of the country in a two–party democracy. One of the important roles of this Chairman, in addition to being the chief executive of the state, chief diplomat and the commander in chief, is being the facilitator of the NPRC.

All elections to the NPRC, the state governorship, the local chairmanship and local councillorship are held every 5 years for a 6– year term while elections to the National and state legislatures are held every 4 years for a 5–year term to provide for an orderly transfer of power in each case. In each case of these two groups of elections, primary and general, a one day election utilizing a one ballot–box system can suffice. All Congressmen are elected officials from their local government areas (LGA) and political party affiliation in a two– party democracy. Each LGA is entitled to two representatives, one to the Senate and the other to the House of Representatives. To facilitate political access and participation, there can be more than one ticket during the primaries alone in which the ticket with a simple majority vote will represent and produce a winning party in the general elections.

There is a need to discuss campaign funding in the electoral process. As can be accepted, money corruption is the root of all evil in Nigeria's political process. The problem was cited as a factor in the June 1993 Presidential election as well as in 1980s Shagari's administration. To prevent money corruption, political candidates can benefit from matching grants between credible candidates of good will and their respective parties. The role of the National Electoral Commission (NEC) should include determining the funding ratios, investigating funding source and fraud of political campaigns, and limiting the amount of monies to be spent by candidates in any election.

How should the NPRC be formed? Each party from each state in a two–party (SDP and NRC) democracy must register names of three candidates with its State and National Party Committee where tickets and the platforms are screened using three main criteria: party philosophy, state/national goals, and candidates personal qualification and credentials to determine candidates for the state governorship, lieutenant governorship and an alternate to represent the state in the NPRC following the outcome of the general election. It is also important that all tickets and platforms be registered with the NEC.

In Nigeria, there should be 4 major political institutions, distinct but connected in the principle of self–government. They are the Constitution, the Supreme Court, the NPRC, and the Congress which comprises the Senate and the House of Representatives. The responsibility of the NPRC is to carry out a public policy which has been signed into law by the chairman of the NPRC. The Supreme Court is the highest court of the land whose duty is to interpret the policy based on its constitutionality, while the legislative body (Senate and House of Representatives) is to legislate, i.e. introduce a bill, educate the public through debate and voting to reject or pass the legislation. (The operation of the U.S. government is a good example concerning the conduct of and the mix between the three branches of government. Winter and Bellows (1981, 239), who described the intricacy of government, stated that:

> Contemporary political systems are more politicked because of a tendency to regard government as having responsibilities in most areas of human concern (environment, inflation, defense, education, retirement, benefits and so forth). In participatory political system government devotes a majority of their time to negotiating and balancing the claims and counterclaims of diverse ideas and groups demanding an official response or opposing a proposed response....A democratically elected legislature is directly and frequently accountable to the people...

The process of enacting a bill into law is an important one. It is based on the constitution and the rule of law. Much attention should be paid to the balance of power between the Judicial, the Executive, and the Legislative branches of government. After a piece of legislation has been duly debated and voted upon by the legislators, it must be signed into law by the chairman of NPRC. What is the specific role of the NPRC members? They're to be the chairman's cabinet. Each member of the NPRC is a head of government in charge of a civil service portfolio such as department of Finance, Agriculture, Education, Mines and Power, etc. and are collectively responsible to ensure the functioning of the machines of government. All department heads are appointed in the spirit of by–partisanship by the chairman of NPRC. This means they are appointed from the party in power in order to inject an element of accountability and competition into the two–party democracy to attest each party's performance, while all assistant department heads are appointed from the minority party to provide checks and balances between the parties at operational levels of government. To further achieve efficiency in government, all appointments should be based on the appointee's pertinent experience and credential. Nothing should therefore prevent appointments of department heads from the minority party in the absence of qualified people from the majority party.

To maintain continuity in government, members of the federal supreme court are appointed for life by the Chairman of the NPRC and confirmed by the Congress. The Chairman and Vice Chairman of the NPRC are selected to hold office for two terms only, i.e. if their party continues to win in the general election. The preferred selection process is the lotto conducted by a Federal Supreme Judge.

THE MILITARY IN NIGERIA'S FUTURE DEMOCRACY

For democracy to survive in Nigeria, the one last hurdle it must face and overcome is the adjustment difficulties of Nigeria's Armed Forces to meet the necessary prerequisites for acceptable military conduct in a democracy. The implication is that the mechanism of democracy, such as people' power, partisanship, and the balance of power between the three branches of government, should be allowed to prevent government from collapsing. An effective civilian police must be trained and put in place to empower citizens to participate in government. Some people have believed that after so many years in

NIGERIA: FLOW CHART OF FEDERALISM
AND BALANCE OF POWER

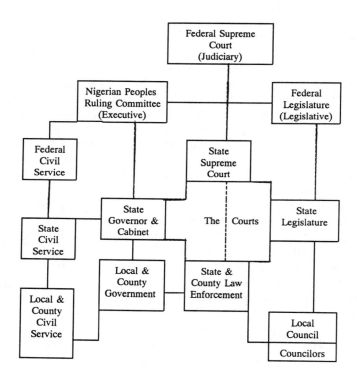

Nigeria: Future Federalism in a Two-Party Democracy

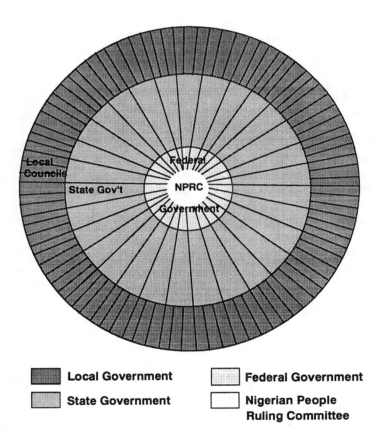

▓ Local Government	░ Federal Government
▒ State Government	☐ Nigerian People Ruling Committee

power, Nigeria's military might have lost its composure of being an effective adjunct to a civilian government; and that nothing can be done to obligate them to leave power voluntarily. Others have however held an opposite view, believing that since the military is usually known for discipline, hierarchical formation and esprit de corps, achieving any necessary adjustments to meet the needs of the society would be as easy as A–B–C. In general, there are two contrasting viewpoints associated with the role of the military in society, especially in Africa. The first viewpoint is that espoused by Mobutu Sese Seko of Zaire, an African despot whose statement that 'though there is a political discontinuity in Congo, there must be military continuity' is almost becoming the modus operandi in the post colonial Africa. The reverse viewpoint is that which suggests that 'a soldier's duty is to follow orders and not to engage in politics' (National Youth Service Corp., p.194).

There is one other important point to be made about the military in society. Members of the military force are citizens of their societies who are equally interested in the well being of their societies. But, because "interests" and "abilities" are generally two different things, a division of labor is often emphasized as a useful tool to accomplish multiple tasks in society. In a practical sense, it can be argued that the military's skills, abilities and lifestyles, outside its specified roles, are incompatible with democratic ideals and the spirit of free enterprise.

However, many examples can be cited where ex–military leaders have demonstrated prominence in partisan politics worldwide. In a literate civilian life, freedom of speech, freedom of the press and expression, freedom of movement, freedom of choice, freedom to ask questions when orders are given and freedom of free election are all basic preconditions to social freedom and economic prosperity, which often times go hand in hand. These indices of freedom are usually compromised in a military run government. Such an argument is supported by the huge contrast in economic prosperity between countries like the United States, West Germany, France, Italy, Australia, Switzerland, Great Britain, to name a few where there are democratic governments and other countries like North Korea, China, Vietnam, Afghanistan, Bhutan, Burma, Iran, Cuba, Iraq, former USSR, and most African countries whose powers are vested in military juntas. It is in this regard that history, while recognizing military leaders like Haile Salassie of Ethiopia, Nassar of Egypt, Fidel Castro of Cuba, Joseph Stalin of Russia, Adolf Hitler of Germany as great nationalists and soldiers in their own right, may deny them the same recognition for

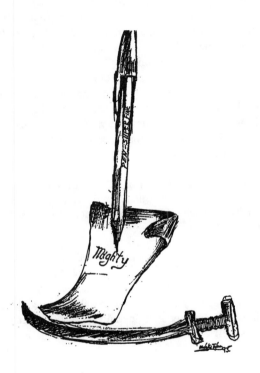

A **PEN** is mightier than a *sword*...

their failure to lay a sound economic, social and political groundwork in their nations.

For more than 20 years, Nigeria has been ruled by a military regime whose illegitimate power base has failed to transform Nigeria economically and politically; its people left looking down in desperation. Like in the colonial days, the people of Nigeria are helpless but not naive. They have, however, recognized the similarity existing between colonial and post–colonial Nigeria. They are not naive because they understand the injustice done to them by their native leaders. They are helpless because since independence they have not fully participated in the government that is supposed to serve them and above all dismayed because their economy is determined by the forces greater than them.

While complete national disintegration has been abated by the military rule in Nigeria, it has been seen as having a destabilizing effect in the Nigerian polity through a system of successive military coup d'etat. Why? This phenomenon was simply explained by Huntington (1968, 242) when he stated:

> if a regime does not develop a political structure which institutional–
> izes some principles of legitimacy, the result can only be a military
> oligarchy in which power is passed among the oligarchies by means
> of coup d'etat.

Contrary to some viewpoints, supporting military dictatorship in politics, it is worth pointing out, that an efficient military organization and its so called interest comparable with civilians' interests for a stable government in society alone do not usually predict the military's future performance in the economic and political arenas. David Lamb described specific situations in Nigeria under the civilian and military rule and stated that:

> the country's oil revenue was squandered in the biggest spending
> binge any African country ever went on. The soldiers came to power
> and proved themselves more corrupt and less efficient than the
> civilians they had overthrown for their corruption and inefficiency
> (Lamb 1987, 301).

There is a difference between combat readiness based on discipline and esprit de corps and the readiness to govern,. particularly in a nation like Nigeria where there are 118 million people with diverse ethnic backgrounds. The very notion itself that a military rule can substitute for a civilian governance is not only inconsistent with the basic principles of democracy but also a misleading proposition considering the demands of the twentieth century geopolitics. Consequently, a statement made by Prof. Abdullahi Smith might have been made in error, or guided by the event of the moment when he stated in Zaira many years ago that "the record of human experience does not lend support to the theory that the civilian always controlled the military" (National Youth Service Corp, p.192). Contrary to Prof. Smith's beliefs, modern history can show that the most prosperous and stable nations are those whose military take orders from the civilian president in a democratic process.

Today, after the Cold War, more countries than ever are democratic and are reaping the benefits therefrom. In an article entitled: More Democracies Than Ever Dot the Globe, But Many are Fragile (Kaplan 1994, A23) stated that "60 percent of the world's 191 nations are now formal democracies, double the number Freedom House found during surveys in the 1970s." From North American to South American, Western Europe, Eastern Europe, Asia to Africa, the old admiration for an iron hand military totalitarianism has ebbed due to its poor taste and inability to satisfy today's human needs. For example, on December 10, 1994, Cuba was excluded from a summit of all Americas' democracies on trade and economic cooperation because of its longstanding military dictatorship. In that summit, Goshko and Behr (1994, A1) reported that "...33 other Western Hemisphere nations pledged today to turn the entire region into the world's largest free trade zone, setting 2005 as the deadline...."

Cuba and Nigeria have two things in common needing change. They are both poor and under dictatorial regimes. With specific emphasis to Nigeria, it is the "people of Nigeria," not the military or corrupt individuals, who should have the sole and legitimate power to change their government. The familiar concept of government of the people, by the people and for the people which has served many great countries well should be adopted in Nigeria. This basic principle has been the cornerstone of most successful democracies worldwide. In the United States for example, the concept of "people's power" is not only the norm of behavior of every citizen including the military but also an embodiment of its constitution (1789) which begins as follows:

> We the People of the United States in order to form a more perfect Union, establish justice, insure domestic Tranquility, provide for the common defense, promote the general Welfare and secure the Blessing of Liberty to ourselves and our Posterity, do ordain and establish this Constitution for the United States of America. . .

In most democracies, the military usually belongs to the ministry (department) of defense, comparable with other functional ministries in society – all of which are managed by individual cabinet members who report to and take orders from their national leader. In most young democracies, however, such as in the First and Second Nigerian Republics, "The function of. . .Nigerian Army, Nigerian Navy and Nigerian Air Force whose responsibility is the defense of the Nation as well as internal security" was grossly misinterpreted. Let us examine what the opening statement of the U.S. Constitution says in this regard. In that constitution the phrase "provide a common defense" may mean that all citizens must consent (through their political representatives in Congress) before the military, subject to the civilian president's (the commander in chief) instructions, can be deployed. This is where the much professed general discipline in the military has served committed democracies well but has totally eluded the fragile ones.   The above analysis explains the fact that in a democracy the military is not above the law. Accordingly, if the Nigerian ministry of defense, i.e. the military, can clandestinely take over the country and hold it hostage, it can also expect the other ministries to do the same even though this capability is seldom exercised but not impossible. Over the years, the biggest demise of Nigeria has been caused by the career civil servants who, by playing their traditional role of sustaining the machine of government, have continued to nurture the mediocrity of Nigeria's career politicians and military dictators. Of course, in most third world countries, fear of intimidation by the military usually misleads the civilian population into believing that only the military can maintain order in society. Nothing can be further from the truth.

Maintaining order in society is a collective venture in which citizens must have the freedom to cooperate. It involves citizens' exercise of "conscience" which is "that quality in man that stands up to authority, law, society and all outside influences, and sees something fresh behind old truth" (Fabry, 1975, 89). Order without social values such as democracy, economic prosperity, social justice, health, security, education and other social amenities is as disastrous as no order at all. Merril (1969) stated that:

Social values, then, play a central role in social problems. Values are normative beliefs pertaining to the important relationship of a society and embodied in its institutional structure...these values are the very stuff of human life, and any threat to them, real or imagined involves serious consequences for the individual and society alike (pp. 418–19).

In fact, such have already been experienced in parts of Africa where children do not get proper nutrition, live in sanitary environments or receive adequate education. For these societies to prosper and avoid self destruction, it seems unwise to use military means in trying to solve problems which are socio–political and economic in nature. Instead, all functional arms of government in society ought to be adequately coordinated and managed to produce citizens' socio–economic well-being.

Socio–economic well–being in citizenry has been known to be essential in encouraging not only good faith political participation but also in effectuating stability in partisan politics. This assertion is contained in many human capital literature which were referred to in the preceding pages of this text. In short, what a nation like Nigeria does not need is a military run government but a government which embodies men and women who are morally committed to end the status quo. The overall goal of Nigeria, therefore, should be that of achieving socio–political stability and economic prosperity at home, and its competitiveness within the context of the 20th century geopolitics.

Summary and Comments

This research work was motivated by such reasons that Nigeria, the richest and the most populous nation in Black Africa, has "gone through numerous political crises since her [sic] Independence from British colonialists in 1960" (Adedibu 1994, 1), and also "the need for the country to move forward. . .to put a stop to the current aimlessness and drift the Nation is currently mired in" (Fayemiwo 1994,10). With the above statements, Adedibu and Fayemiwo seemed to have taken words out of our mouth by their emphasis on Nigeria's wrong direction since self-rule in 1960. Our goal was to investigate and document some of the causes for Nigeria's social, political and economic decay and make recommendations which can be helpful in national building.

Nigeria is a nation of many people, divided by tribal and ethnic lines and whose different roots, early associations and settlements, folkways, religion and other foreign influences are traced into historic times. As a practical matter of our time, such division should not necessarily mean divisiveness. In the minds of many people globally, Nigeria with its natural resources and human potential is expected to be well-to-do economically, but tribal politics has done irreparable damage, making it one of the poorest nations on earth. Today, Nigerians are still looking for that Moses to lead them to the promised land, so to speak (see Holy Bible, Exodus 14:1-31).

Presented in this book is a documentary of continued disillusionment in Nigeria, perpetuated first by those who invaded and corrupted its tradition, usurped its wealth in many ways for many years and left the country in ruin; second by the indigenous Nigerian leaders who took over Nigeria after Independence in 1960 and, having behaved like the colonialists, have corrupted it too. Nigeria is ultimately viewed as a nation in transition and with a lot of obstacles to overcome every step of the way.

To determine who has caused the most harm to Nigeria to date, the colonialists or the Nigerian leaders, is the subject of much debate. We hope the information we have provided thus far can help in the event of such debates. In the meantime, it is apparent that much of the blame which usually goes to the colonialists for their economic and political atrocities in Nigeria are somewhat outmoded. The focus of blame today in such matters ought to rest squarely on the shoulders of Nigerian leaders, who in spite of the abundance of time, natural resources and human capital in their favor after Independence, failed to transform Nigeria for the best. After all, Nigerian leaders are expected to have a higher moral responsibility than the colonialists in building their country.

To move in a positive direction into the future, one must first seek an understanding and the truth about the past and the present. Therefore, the precolonial, colonial, and postcolonial activities in Nigeria as presented here have constituted the basis for such understanding and truth. Postcolonial Nigeria as in colonial days has been marred by tribalism, corruption, greed, elitism, division by language, religion, ethnicity and lack of moral leadership. These are also factors which have remained instrumental in Nigeria's political and economic destruction and tribal disunity. Unless these fundamental threats to national unity are overcome, there is no reason to concern ourselves with the concept of Nigeria merely as a geographical entity. National integration as well as Nigeria's democracy is a necessity, and much of the recommendations contained in this text, if implemented in good faith, could move Nigeria closer to achieving the much needed political stability, ethnic integration and socioeconomic prosperity. David Lamb in *The Africans* also saw Nigeria's social, political and economic evolution in almost the same light when he stated that:

> many formidable challenges lie ahead for Nigeria. Will the soldiers stay in the barracks if the civilians falter? Can oil really be put to work to benefit the majority instead of a chosen few? Will tribalism again surface as the most powerful force? Can corruption and greed be contained and national energies channeled toward common goals? These may remain unanswered questions for years to come but the most encouraging sign I think that the Nigerian experiment will succeed is the presence of a growing middle and upper class. It is the

largest, most substantial one in Black Africa, and it is certainly worth remembering that it was the birth of the English middle class in the sixteenth and seventeenth centuries that enabled Britain to become stable and powerful (Lamb 1987, p. 312).

Bibliography

Adedibu, Lamidi. (1994). Can June 12 Lead to a Civil War of Disintegration of Nigeria? *Razor*, May 31, p.1.

_____. (1994). African Political Systems. *Africa Demos, Vol. III, Number 3, September*. p.27.

_____. (1992). Africa: Dispelling the Myth. Washington D.C.:*Washington Office on Africa for the Africa Peace Tour* (WOA), p.1.

_____. (1994). "Africa 1994: Ecstasy and Agony. *Africa Demos*, Vol. III, No. 3, September, p.1.

Agbaje, Adigun. (1994). Beyond the Generals: Twilight of Democracy in Nigeria. *Africa Demos*, Vol. III, Number 3, September, p.4.

_____. (1971). Aid to Bible Understanding. *Watchtower*. New York:Bible and Tract Society of New York, Inc.

Aigbogun, Frank. (1994). Nigerian Dictator Fires Three Labor Union Leaders.*The Washington Post*, Thursday, August 18, p. A13.

Anderson, Richard C., & Gaust, Gerald W. (1973). *Educational Psychology: The Science of Instruction and Learning*

Anyanwu, Chris. (1993). What Injustice Does to A Man. *The Sunday Magazine*, October 3, pp. 12–20.

172   *Democracy and Ethnic Diversity in Nigeria*

Ayeni, Olugbenga. (1992). "Presidency for Sale?" *West Africa.* August 17–23, p. 1386.

Babarinsa, Dare., Mohammed, Yakubu., Akinrinade, Soji., Oladepo, Wale., Mba Janet., Ben, Victor. (1990) "Load Shedding: The Military is in the Grip of Retirement Fever as Generals Bow Out Compulsorily. Newswatch. Vol. 12, No. 12, Sept. 17, p.15.

Bakare, Idowu. (1994). Nigeria: Record of Contradictions. *National Concord,* Tuesday, January 18, p. A1.

Banks, James A. (1979). *Teaching Strategies For Ethnic Studies,* Second Edition. Boston: Allyn and Bacon, Inc.

Brooks, Geraldine. (1994). Shells Nigerian Fields Produce Few Benefits for Regions Villagers: Despite Huge Oil Revenues, Firm and Government Neglect the Impoverished. *The Wall Street Journal,* Friday, May 6, p. A1.

Buckley, Stephen (1995) Nigeria Suffers in Silence. *The Washington Post,* Monday, April 3, A1.

Buckley, Stephen. (1995). After 35 Years, Nigeria Still Stumbling on Road to Democracy. *Washington Post,* Sunday, October 1, p.A28.

Clarke, Henrick John, & ben–Jochannan, Yosef. (1991). *New Dimensions in African History.* New Jersey: Africa World Press, Inc.

Cohen, Hermon J. (1994). The Private Sector and Democracy in Africa, *African Business Report; The Quarterly Journal of the African Business Round Table – North America,* Vol.1, No.2, Oct., p.5.

Coleman, James C., & Broen, William E. (1972). *Abnormal Psychology and Modern Life,* Fourth Edition. London: Scott, Foresman and Company.

Coleman, James S. (1958). *Nigeria: Background to Nationalism.* Berkley, CA: University of California Press.

Connelly, Philip, & Perlman, Robert. (1975). *The Politics of Scarcity: Resource Conflict in International Relations*. London: Oxford University Press.

Daramy, Batu Sheikh. (1983). *Colonialism and the Underdevelopment of Sierra Leone 1918–1967*. Unpublished Master's Thesis, Howard University, Washington, D.C.

Davidson, Basil, Buah F K, Ajayi J FA. (1965). *The Growth of African Civilization: A History of West Africa 1000–18005*. London: Longman Group, Ltd.

_____. (1990) *Debt: A Crisis For Development*. United Nations, Department of Public Information.

Diop, Cheihk Anta. (1987). *Precolonial Black Africa: A Comparative Study of the Political and Social Systems of Europe and Black Africa From Antiquity to the Formation of Modern States*. New York: Lawrence Hill Books.

_____. (1958). *Encyclopedia America: The International Reference Work*. New York: American Corporation Eze, Ayogu. (1992). "Bleak Christmas." Newswatch, vol. 13, No. 2, January 7, p. 9.

Fabry, Joseph B. (1975). *The Pursuit of Meaning*. Dublin, The Mercier Press.

Fayemiwo, Moshood. (1994). Nigeria's Future Decided on June 12,1994: Civil War and Disintegration Loom as... *Razor*, May 31, p. 10.

Faul, Michael. (1993). Bribery Claims Increase Against Nigerian Leader. *The Washington Times*, Monday, August 16, p. A9.

Faul, Michael. (1993). Nigeria Nullifies Election: U.S. Suspends Aid As Army Blocks Civilian Takeover. *The Washington Times*, Monday, August 16, p. A9.

Faul, Michael. (1993). Democracy is Still Elusive in Nigeria. *The Washington Times*, Monday, June 28, p. A11.

Felder. Cain Hooe (ed). (1993). *The Original African Heritage Study Bible: The King James Version.* Nashville, Tenn: The Jarnes C. Winston Publishing Company.

Fremantle, Anne (ed). (1962). *Mao Tse Tung: An Anthology of His Writing.* New York: The American Library.

Friere, Paulo. (1973). *Education for Critical Consciousness.* New York: The Continuum Publishing Company.

Fritz, Mark. (1993). 11 Die as Nigeria's Rioters Protest Military Rule. *The Washington Post,* Wednesday, July 7, p. A23.

_____. (1963). *Funk and Wagnalls Standard College Dictionary.* New York: Harcourt, Brace and World, Inc.

Gans, Herbert J. (1992). Fighting the Biases Embedded in Social Concepts of the Poor. *The Chronicle of Higher concepts of the Poor.* The Chronicle of Higher Education, January 8, p. A56.

Garvey, Marcus. (1986). *The Philosophy and Opinions of Mareua Garvey: Or, Africa for the Africans.* Dover, Massachusetts: The Majority Press.

Goliber, Thomas J. (1989). Africa's Expanding Population: Old Problems, New Policies. *Population Bulletin,* Yol. 44, No. 3, Population Reference Bureau, Inc.

Goshko, John M., & Behr, Peter. (1994). Leaders of Western Hemisphere Agree to Form Free Trade Zone. *The Washington Post,* Sunday, December 11, p. A1.

Gregor, James A. (1968). *Contemporary Radical Ideologies: Totalitarian Thoughts in the Twentieth Century.* New York: Random House.

_____. *Guidelines for the Fourth National Development Plan 1981–85.* Federal Republic of Nigeria, Lagos, The Federal Ministry of National Planning.

Haines, Grove C. (ed). (1955). *Africa Today.* Baltimore: The John Hopkins Press.

Halford, John. (1994). The Challenge of Africa. *The Plain Truth: A Magazine of Understanding*, Vol. 59, No. 10, November/December, p. 9.

Hamacheck, Don E. (1978). *Encounter With The Self.* Second Edition. New York: Holt, Rinehart and Winston.

Hall, Calvin S., & Lidsay, Gardner. (1978). *Theories of Personality.* Third Edition. New York: John Wiley and Sons.

Harris, Joseph E. (1972). *Africans and Their History.* Revised Edition. New York: Penguin Books USA, Inc.

Hartfield, Mark 0. (1971). *Conflict and Conscience*, Texas, World Book, Publishers.

Hilgard, Emest R. (1953). *Introduction to Psychology.* New York: Harcourt, Brace and Company.

Hodgkins, Thomas. (1957). Nationalism in Colonial Africa. New York: University Press, Inc.

_____. (1994). Hope Betrayed: Retired Brigadier General David Mark, Former Minister of Communications in an Interview with Newswatch Charges that the Abacha Coup is a Departure from the Original Plan. Excerpts *Newswatch*, April 11, p. 10.

Howard, Rhoda E. (1986). *Human Rights in Commonwealth Africa.* New Jersey: Rowman & Littlefield Publishers.

Huntington, Samuel P. (1968). *Political Order in Changing Societies.* New Haven: Yale University Press.

_____. *Illiterate Population*, Statistical Yearbook UNESCO.

Jacob, Yusuph. (1994). Mistrust Threatens Nigeria's Unity. *National Concord*, Monday, January 24, p. 11.

Jung, John. (1978). *Understanding Human Motivation: A Cognitive Approach.* New York: MacMillan Publishing Co., Inc.

Kalu, Egwuonwu U. (1994). "Committee of Concerned Delegates: National Constitutional Conference" *The Washington Post*, Thursday, October 27, p. A28.

Kaplan, Refet. (1994). More Democracies than Ever Dot Globe, but Many are Fragile. *The Washington Times*, Friday, December 16, p. A23.

Keesing, Rogers M. (1976). *Cultural Anthropology: A Contemporary Perspective.* New York: Holt, Rinehart and Winston.

Kirk–Green, A. (1971). *Crisis and Conflict in Nigeria: A Documentary Source Book 1966–1970, Vol. 1.* London: Oxford University Press.

Kneller, George F. (1971). *Foundations of Education.* Third Edition, New York: John Wiley and Sons.

Krech, David, Crutchfield Richard, & Ballachey, Egerton L. (1962). *Individual in Society: A Textbook of Social Psychology.* New York: McGraw–Hill Book Company, Inc.

Lamb, David. (1987). *The Africans.* New York: Vantage Books – A Division of Random House.

Lau, James B. (1975). *Behavior in Organization: An Experiential Approach.* Homewood, Illinois: Richard D. Irwin, Inc.

Lumumba, Patrice. (1978). *Patrice Lumumba.* London: Panat Books, Limited.

Makanju, Ayo. (1994). Only Democracy Can Save Economy. *National Concord, Vol. 14*, Wednesday, January 26, p. 1.

Marden, Charles F. & Meyer, Gladys. (1978). *Minorities in American Society,* Fifth Edition. New York: D. Van Nostrand Company.

Maslow, A.H. (1954). *Motivation and Personality*. New York: Harper and Row.

Mazrui, Ali A. (1986). *The Africans: A Triple Heritage*. Boston: Little, Brown and Company.

McCaskie, T.C. (1994). *Nigeria: Recent History. Africa South of the Sahara*, 23rd Edition. London: Europa Publication Ltd.

Merril, Francis E. (1969). *Society and Culture: An Introduction to Sociology*, Fourth Edition. New Jersey: Prentice-Hall, Inc.

Morse, Joseph Laffan (ed). (1970). *Funk and Wagnalls Standard Reference Encyclopedia, Vols. 1-18*. New York: Standard Reference Library, Inc.

Myrdal, Gunner. (1960). *Beyond the Welfare State: Economic Planning and Its International Implication*. New Haven: Yale University Press.

_____. National Universities Commission. *Nigeria Annual Report*. January 1989–December 1989.

_____. (1973). *National Youth Service Corps: Lectures for the Orientation Course*. Federal Republic of Nigeria.

_____. (1994). Nigeria Resumes Democratic Process, Guarantees Press Freedom and Intensifies War Against Drug Trafficking. Embassy of Nigeria, Washington, D.C. *The Washington Post*, Monday, May 2, p. D20.

_____. (1993). Nigerian Moves to Retain Power. *The Washington Times*, Saturday, August 7, p. A9.

_____. (1992) "Nigeria Suspends Political Activity: Run-off Primary Vote Postponed. *Associated Press Report. The Washington Post*. Thursday, October 8, p. A36.

Nkrumuh, Kwame. (1970). *Class Struggle in Africa*. New York: International Publishers Co., Inc.

Democracy and Ethnic Diversity in Nigeria

Nyerere, Julius (1974). *Freedom and Development: A Selection from Writing and Speeches 1968–73*, New York, Oxford University Press.

Obasanjo, Olusegun. (1990). *Not My Will*. Ibadan University Press Limited.

Okie, Susan. (1994). Aids Devouring Africa Even As Awareness Grows. *The Washington Post*, Thursday, August 18, p. A29.

Okoh, Wilfred. (1994). *Rationale for the Two Year Rotational Presidency in Nigeria: Epigenesis in Constitutional Evolution.* An unpublished document, Washington, D.C., March 29, p. 3.

Orwell, George. (1946). *Animal Farm: A Fairy Story by George Orwell*. New York: Harcourt, Brace, Javanovich, Inc.

Paul, Joseph, Esu. (____). *Current Affairs: Nigeria's 30 States and 589 Councils.* P.O. Box 1002, Nigeria, Markurdi – Benue State, JEP Group of Publishers and Advertisers Limited.

Parmele, Jennifer. (1994). Losing the Race to Feed Its People: Africa's Population Grows Faster Than Its Crops. *The Washington Post*, Wednesday, August 24, p. A23.

Parrinder, Geoffery. (1978). *West African Religion: A Study of the Beliefs and Practices of Akan, Ewe, Yoruba, Ibo and Kindred Peoples.* London: Epworth Press.

Richburg, Keith B. (1994). Rwanda Wrecked by Ethnic Violence: Rampages Follow President's Assassination. *The Washington Post*, Friday, April 8, p. A1.

Richburg, Keith. (1992). Will African Democracy Work? *The Washington Post*, Sunday, August 16, p. C5.

Richburg, Keith B. (1992). Asia and Africa: The Roots of Success and Despair (Two Regions of High Economic Potential Took Divergent Paths After Independence). *The Washington Post*, Sunday, July 12, p. A26.

Rodney, Walter, (1972). *How Europe Underdeveloped Africa.* Great Britain: Bogle–L'Ouverture Publications,

Rogers, C.R. (1959). *A Theory of Therapy, Personality, and Interpersonal Relationship as Developed in the Client–Centered Framework...* New York: McGraw–Hill Book Company, Inc.

Ross, Murray G. (1956). *Community Organization: Theory and Principles.* New York: Harper and Brother Publishers.

Sanda, A.O. (1992). *Lectures on the Sociology of Development.* Lagos: Fact Finders International.

Schott, Richard L. (1974). *The Bureaucratic State: The Evolution and Scope of the American Federal Bureaucracy.* New Jersey: General Learning Press.

Seybolt, Peter J. (1983). *Through Chinese Eyes.* Revised Edition, Vol. 1, New York: A Cite Book.

Shiner, Cindy. (1994). Scanning Gullible Americans is a Well–Oiled Industry in Nigeria. *The Washington Post*, Tuesday, August 30, p. A15.

Shiner, Cindy. (1994). Nigerian Opposition Leader Charged With Treason. *The Washington Post*, Thursday, July 7, p. A13.

Smith, Patrick. (1990). Nigeria Adjustment's New Phase, Africa Recovery. *United Nations, Department of Public Information, Vol. 4, April–June,* pp. 6–7.

Smith, Patrick. (1994). *Nigeria: Economy. Africa South of the Sahara,* 23rd Edition. London: Europa Publications, LTD.

Srnivasan, Iyra. (1983). *Perspectives on Nonformal Adult Learning: Functional Education for Individual Community and National Development.* Boston: World Education, Inc.

Taylor, Paul. (1994). First Black President of South Africa Praises Predecessors – Military. *The Washington Post*, Wednesday, May 10, p. A1.

_____. *The Constitution of the United States of America.* U.S. Government. Washington D.C.: U.S. Government Printing Office.

_____. (1986). *The World Book Encyclopedia, Vol. 13.* Chicago: World Book, Inc.

_____. (1989). *The New Lexicon Webster's Dictionary of the English Language*, 1989 Edition. New York: Lexicon Publication, Inc.

_____. (1987). The Secretary General Report on The Implementation of the Africa Recovery Programme: A Summary. *Africa Recovery News Feature.* United Nations, Department of Public Information, p. 3.

_____. (1968). *The Nigerian School Directory.* Lagos: John West Publication Limited.

Ugochukwu, Oneyma. (1986). Nigeria: Babangida Keeps Going. *West Africa*, July 28, p. 1567.

Umoren, Joseph Aaron. (1989). *A Study of Factors Related to the Educational Decision and Career Plans...* Ph.D. Dissertation. The American University, Washington, D.C.: University Microfilm International, A Bell & Howell Information Company.

Waidor–Pregbagha, Stevie. (1994). This is Genocide: The Ogoni Cry Out. *Tell*, January 31, No. 5, p. 10.

_____. (1971). *Webster's Seventh New Collegiate Dictionary.* Massachusetts: G & C Meriam Company.

William, Chancelor. (1987). *The Destruction of Black Civilization: Great Issues of Race from 4500 B.C. to 2000 AD,.* Chicago: Third World Press.

Winter, Herbert R. & Bellows, Thomas J. (1981). *People and Politics: An Introduction to Political Science*, Second Edition. New York: John Wiley & Sons.

Wrightsmen, Lawrence S. (1972). *Social Psychology of the Seventies*. Monterey, California: Book/Cole Publishing Company.

_____. (1990). *World Population Data Sheet*. Population Reference Bureau, Inc. (PRB), Washington, D.C. 20009, USA.

Index